Evaluating
Electronic Portfolios
in Teacher Education

A volume in
Research Methods in Educational Technology
Walter F. Heinecke, *Series Editor*

Evaluating Electronic Portfolios in Teacher Education

Edited by

Pete Adamy
University of Rhode Island

Natalie B. Milman
The George Washington University

SCHOOL OF EDUCATION
CURRICULUM LABORATORY
UM-DEARBORN

INFORMATION AGE PUBLISHING, INC.
Charlotte, NC • www.infoagepub.com

Library of Congress Cataloging-in-Publication Data

Evaluating electronic portfolios in teacher education / edited by Pete Adamy, Natalie B. Milman.
   p. cm. – (Research methods in educational technology)
 Includes bibliographical references.
 ISBN 978-1-60752-031-3 (pbk.) – ISBN 978-1-60752-032-0 (hardcover) 1. Teachers–Training of. 2. Electronic portfolios in education. I. Adamy, Pete. II. Milman, Natalie B.
 LB1728.E93 2008
 371.14'4–dc22

                                                  2008037768

Printed in the United States of America

CONTENTS

INTRODUCTION

Natalie Milman
George Washington University

Pete Adamy
University of Rhode Island

Teaching portfolios—compilations of professional materials that present a "structured documentary history of a set of coached or mentored acts of teaching, substantiated by samples of student portfolios" (Shulman, 1998, p. 37)—are growing in popularity as a means for assessing the competence of both inservice teachers and preservice teacher candidates. Such performance-based approaches, especially in light of school districts' needs to demonstrate that their teachers are "highly qualified" (No Child Left Behind Act) provide a richer and more accurate portrait of a teacher's competence, especially when compared to simplistic approaches to assessing teacher competency such as the PRAXIS. Portfolios can help teacher educators and district level personnel move away from simple check-off assignments or multiple-choice standardized tests for demonstrating a teacher's knowledge and competence about teaching. Portfolios' popularity may also be growing in part because teaching portfolios promote professional knowledge development (Mokhtari, Yellin, Bull, & Montgomery, 1996; Zidon, 1996), professional growth (Dietz, 1995; Green & Smyser, 1996; Wray, 2001), and reflective thinking and practice (Borko, Michalec, Timmons, & Siddle, 1997; Davies & Willis, 2001; Dietz, 1995; Jackson, 1998; Loughran

Evaluating Electronic Portfolios in Teacher Education, pages vii–xiii
Copyright © 2009 by Information Age Publishing

& Corrigan, 1995; Lyons, 1998a; Lyons, 1998b; Reis, 2002; Stroble, 1995; Wade & Yarbrough, 1996), all of which are important components to teacher professional development.

It is also likely a result of the accreditation/re-accreditation process for schools, colleges, and departments of education (SCDE's). Although only half of SCDE's with teacher education programs are accredited by the National Council for Accreditation of Teacher Education (NCATE), they are responsible for training seventy-five percent of the nation's new teachers (Darling Hammond, Pacheco, Michelli, LePage, Hammerness, & Youngs, 2005). In developing their accreditation standards, NCATE incorporated the Interstate New Teacher Assessment and Support Consortium's (INTASC) performance-based Model Standards for Beginning Teacher Licensing, Assessment and Development (INTASC, 1992). The development of the INTASC standards was heavily influenced by the performance-based standards of the National Board for Professional Teaching Standards. (Darling-Hammond et al, 2005). This means that approximately three quarters of the nation's new teachers are trained in programs that evaluate their performance through outcomes-based performance assessments. This movement towards performance-based assessment has been accompanied by the adoption of portfolios for assessment by almost 90% of SCDE's (Salzman, Denner, & Harris, 2002).

More recently, those advocating teaching portfolios have begun to capitalize on the use of technology in the development of portfolios. Professional materials included in electronic (or digital) teaching portfolios are presented using a combination of digital media such as audio recordings, graphics, hypermedia programs, database, spreadsheet, video, and word processing software (Kilbane & Milman, 2003, 2005). These teaching portfolios developed and displayed in digital format are often called electronic portfolios, e-folios, digital teaching portfolios, multimedia portfolios, and webfolios (Kilbane & Milman, 2003, 2005). Such portfolios contain content that resembles more conventional teaching portfolios but have unique characteristics that influence their design, production, and sharing.

Electronic portfolios make the NCATE accreditation process much more palatable (reviewers are able to access portfolios online easily), the sharing of portfolios more accessible (web-published portfolios are available to anyone with an Internet-accessible computer), the duplication of portfolios more economical (they may be duplicated on CD for pennies), and the preservation of artifacts more lasting (Kilbane & Milman, 2003, 2005). Therefore, it is no wonder that "[the] term 'electronic portfolio,' or 'ePortfolio,' is on everyone's lips," as Batson (2002) claims. Many consider portfolios in digital format a perfect panacea—"as if this new tool is the answer to all the questions we didn't realize we were asking" (Batson, 2002).

Research conducted within the past few years about electronic portfolios in teacher education shows that there are benefits and challenges to their use and implementation in SCDE's. For example, several studies show that electronic portfolios promote the development of technology skills (Abrami & Barrett, 2005; Bartlett, 2002; Bartlett & Sherry, 2004; Bartlett & Sherry, 2005; Milman, 2005; Milman & Kilbane, 2005; Sherry & Bartlett, 2004–2005;) and reflection (Smits, Wang, Towers, Chrichton, Field, & Tarr, 2005; Tosh, Light, Fleming, & Haywood, 2005; Wilson, Wright, & Stallworth, 2003; Wright, Stallworth, & Ray, 2002). Also, preservice teacher candidates report general positive learning experiences in creating electronic portfolios when they receive accurate information about the purpose of developing electronic portfolios along with adequate support for creating them (Gatlin & Jacob, 2002; Gassner & Mallaun, 2006; Norton-Meier, 2003; Strudler & Wetzel, 2005). However, there are challenges, as well, to implementing electronic portfolios. Several researchers reported that developing an electronic portfolio is time consuming (Milman, 2005; Olsen, Wentworth, & Dimond, 2002; Strudler & Wetzel, 2005; Weiseman, 2004) and also requires specialized technical skill (Milman, 2005)—two factors that might impede their development. And yet, the question: "Do the advantages outweigh the challenges?" clearly needs further examination as Wetzel and Strudler (2006) contend.

More current research (Adamy, 2004; Strudler & Wetzel, 2005, 2006; Tosh, Light, Fleming, & Haywood, 2005; Wetzel & Strudler, 2005a, 2005b, 2006; Wilkerson & Lang, 2003) also highlights the tensions that arise between the needs of schools, colleges, and departments of education in using electronic portfolios as assessment tools, and the needs and purposes of teacher candidates in developing electronic portfolios. As more and more SCDE's require their teacher candidates to develop electronic portfolios, and as more and more of these same institutions begin using these tools as part of the accreditation/re-accreditation process, it is imperative that teacher educators gain a solid understanding about them, especially if they are used for "high stakes" decisions such as whether or not a preservice teacher candidate earns licensure or not.

While research on the effectiveness of electronic portfolios for assessment and accreditation is emerging, many who are now using, or who are beginning to use, electronic portfolios are looking to justify the cost and effort involved. The purposes of this volume are to create an in-depth portrait of ways in which electronic portfolios efforts can be evaluated effectively, and to provide examples of e-folio evaluation in the form of case studies.

In the first chapter, Robert J. Beck and Sharon L. Bear from the University of California, Irvine describe research they conducted that examined the reflective skill development of teacher candidates vis-à-vis both formative and summative portfolios. They found that formative portfolios promoted more reflection than summative ones. Also, they share a model for professional development and reflection using electronic portfolios.

The second chapter, by Arthur Recesso, Michael Hannafin, Feng Wang, Benjamin Deaton, Peter Rich, and Craig Shepherd of the Learning and Performance Support Laboratory at the University of Georgia, introduces the Evidential Reasoning & Decision Making (ERDM) approach as a formative methodology for implementing teacher portfolios.

In chapter three, Andrea Bartlet from the University of Hawai'i at Manoa examines a five-step approach to evaluating electronic teaching portfolios that implements both qualitative and quantitative methodologies.

In chapter four, Bruce Havelock of the RMC Research Corporation explores issues in evaluating electronic portfolios and their implementation. This chapter includes a discussion of using electronic portfolios for "high stakes" accountability systems.

In chapter five, Natalie Milman from The George Washington University presents the results of a mixed method study about electronic portfolios, as well as the implications of applying this methodology to the evaluation of electronic portfolio systems.

Chapter six presents a set of strategies for the evaluation of electronic portfolios in teacher education that focuses on change in individual teachers' practices over time, and is based on the advice offered by the authors of this volume. The intention of these chapters is to serve as models for assessment and evaluation of electronic portfolios in teacher education, as well as to spark further investigations on this tool that is becoming ubiquitous in so many SCDE's across the United States and abroad.

REFERENCES

Abrami, P., & Barrett, H. (2005). Directions for research and development on electronic portfolios. *Canadian Journal of Learning and Technology 31*(3), 1–15.

Adamy, P. (2004). Strategies for enhancing assessment with electronic portfolios. *Journal of Computing in Higher Education*, 15(2), 85–97.

Batson, T. (2002). The electronic portfolio boom: What's it all about? *Campus Technology*. Retrieved September 11, 2006 from http://syllabus.com/article. asp?id=6984

Bartlett. A. (2002). Using electronic portfolios to prepare preservice teachers to implement technology. *International Journal of Learning, 9*, 225–235.

Bartlett, A., & Sherry, A. (2004). Non-technology-savvy preservice teachers' perceptions of electronic teaching portfolios. *Contemporary Issues in Technology and Teacher Education* [Online serial], *4*(2). Available: http://www.citejournal. org/vol4/iss2/currentpractice/article1.cfm

Bartlett, A., & Sherry, A. C. (2005). Two views of electronic portfolios in teacher education: Non-technology undergraduates and technology graduate students. *International Journal of Instructional Media, 33*(3), 245–253.

Borko, H., Michalec, P., Timmons, M., & Siddle, J. (1997, November-December). Student teaching portfolios: A tool for promoting reflective practice. *Journal of Teacher Education, 48*(5), 345–357.

Darling-Hammond, L., Pacheco, A., Michelli, N., LePage, P., Hammerness, K., & Youngs, P. (2005). Implementing curriculum renewal in teacher education: Managing organizational and policy change. In L. Darling-Hammond & J. Bransford (Eds.), *Preparing teachers for a changing world: What teachers should learn and be able to do* (pp. 442–479). San Francisco: Jossey-Bass.

Davies, M. A., & Willis, E. M. (2001). Through the looking glass . . . preservice professional portfolios. *Teacher Educator 37*(1), 27–36.

Dietz, M. (1995). Using portfolios as a framework for professional development. *Journal of Staff Development, 16*, 40–43.

Gassner, O., & Mallaun, J. (2006). Insights from content analysis of digital portfolios in school practice. In C. Crawford, R. Carlsen, I. Gibson, K. McFerrin, J. Price, R. Weber, & D. A. Willis (Eds.) *Technology and teacher education annual* (pp. 2207–2212) Norfolk, VA: Association for the Advancement of Computing in Education.

Gatlin, L., & Jacob, S. (2002). Standards-based digital portfolios: A component of authentic assessment for preservice teachers. *Action in Teacher Education, 23*(4), 28–34.

Green, J., & Smyser, S. (1996). *The teacher portfolio: A strategy for professional development and evaluation.* Lancaster, PA: Technomic.

Interstate New Teacher Assessment and Support Consortium (1992). *Model standards for beginning teacher licensing, assessment, and development: A resource for state dialogue.* Retrieved January 7, 2008, from http://www.ccsso.org/content/pdfs/corestrd.pdf.

Jackson, D. (1998). *Developing student generated computer portfolios.* Paper presented at the ninth annual conference of the Society for Information Technology and Teacher Education, Washington, D.C.

Kilbane, C. R., & Milman, N. B. (2003). *The digital teaching portfolio handbook: A developmental guide for educators.* Boston: Allyn & Bacon.

Kilbane, C. R., & Milman, N. B. (2005). *The digital teaching portfolio workbook: understanding the Digital teaching portfolio development process.* Boston: Allyn & Bacon.

Loughran, J. & Corrigan, D. (1995). Teaching portfolios: A strategy for developing learning and teaching in preservice teacher education. *Teaching and Teacher Education, 11*, 565–577.

Lyons, N. (1998a). Portfolios and their consequences: Developing as a reflective practitioner. In N. Lyons (Ed.), *With portfolio in hand: Validating the new teacher professionalism* (pp. 23–37). New York: Teachers College Press.

Lyons, N. (1998b). Reflection in teaching: Can it be developmental? A portfolio perspective. *Teacher Education Quarterly, 25*(1), 115–127.

Milman, N. B. (2005). Web-based digital teaching portfolios: Fostering reflection and confidence in preservice teacher education students. *Journal of Technology and Teacher Education 13*(3), 373–396.

Milman, N. B., & Kilbane, C. R. (2005). Digital teaching portfolios: Catalysts for fostering authentic professional development. *Canadian Journal of Learning and Technology 31*(3), 51–65.

Mokhtari, K., Yellin, D., Bull, K., & Montgomery, D. (1996, September–October). Portfolio assessment in teacher education: Impact on preservice teachers' knowledge and attitudes. *Journal of Teacher Education, 47*(4), 245–262.

Norton-Meier, L. A. (2003). To efoliate or not to efoliate? The rise of the electronic portfolio in teacher education. *Journal of Adolescent & Adult Literacy, 46*(6), 516–518.

Olsen, R., Wentworth, N., & Dimond, D. (2002, March). *Electronic portfolios in evolution.* Paper presented at the annual meeting of the Society for Information Technology and Teacher Education, Nashville, TN. Retrieved April 19, 2004, from http://www.aace.org/conf/site/pt3/paper_3008_441.pdf

Reis, N. (2002). The benefits, tensions, and visions of portfolios as a wide-scale assessment for teacher education. *Action in Teacher Education 24*(4), 10–17.

Salzman, S., Denner, P., & Harris, L. (2002). *Teaching education outcomes measures: Special study survey.* Paper presented at the Annual Meeting of the American Association of Colleges of Teacher Education, New York, NY. (ERIC Document Reproduction Service No. ED465791)

Sherry, A. C., & Bartlett, A. (2004–2005). Worth of electronic portfolios to education majors: A "two by four" perspective. *Journal of Educational Technology Systems 33*(4), 399–419.

Shulman, L. (1998). Teacher portfolios: A theoretical activity. In Lyons, N. (Ed.), *With portfolio in hand: Validating the new teacher professionalism* (pp. 23–37). New York: Teachers College Press.

Smits, H., Wang, H-C., Towers, J., Chrichton, S., Field, J., & Tarr, P. (2005). Deepening understanding of inquiry teaching and learning with e-portfolios in a teacher preparation program. *Canadian Journal of Learning and Technology 31*(3) 111–119.

Stroble, E. (1995). Portfolio pedagogy: Assembled evidence and unintended consequences. *Teacher Education, 7*(2), 97–102.

Strudler, N., & Wetzel, K. (2005). The diffusion of electronic portfolios in teacher education: Issues of initiation and implementation. *Journal of Research on Technology in Education, 37*(4), 411–433.

Strudler, N., & Wetzel, K. (April, 2006). *Costs and benefits of electronic portfolios in teacher education: Faculty and administrative perspectives.* Paper presented at the Annual Meeting of the American Educational Research Association, San Francisco. CA.

Tosh, D., Light, T. P., Fleming, K., & Haywood, J. (2005). Engagement with electronic portfolios: Challenges from the student perspective. *Canadian Journal of Learning and Technology 31*(3), 89–110.

Wade, R., & Yarbrough, D. (1996). Portfolios: A tool for reflective thinking in teacher education? *Teaching and Teacher Education, 12*, 63–79.

Weiseman, K. (2004). *Mandated standards-based electronic portfolio assessment for measuring preservice teacher quality.* Paper presented at the Annual Meeting of theAmerican Educational Research Association, San Diego, CA.

Wetzel, K., &. Strudler, N. (2005a). A survey of colleges of education thought to be accomplished users of electronic portfolio programs. In C. Crawford, R. Carlsen, I. Gibson, K. McFerrin, J. Price, R. Weber, & D. A. Willis (Eds.) *Technology and teacher education annual* (pp. 208–214). Norfolk, VA: Association for the Advancement of Computing in Education.

Wetzel, K., & Strudler, N. (2005b). The diffusion of electronic portfolios in teacher education: Next steps and recommendations from accomplished users. *Journal of Research on Technology in Education, 38*(2), 231–243.

Wetzel, K., & Strudler, N. (2006). Costs and benefits of electronic portfolios in teacher education: Student voices. *Journal of Computing in Teacher Education, 22*(3), 69–78.

Wilkerson, J. R., & Lang, W. S. (2003, December 3). Portfolios, the Pied Piper of teacher certification assessments: Legal and psychometric issues. *Education Policy Analysis Archives, 11*(45). Retrieved June, 2005 from http://epaa.asu.edu/epaa/v11n45/.

Wilson, E. K., Wright, V. H., & Stallworth, B. J. (2003). Secondary preservice teachers' development of electronic portfolios: An examination of perceptions. *Journal of Technology and Teacher Education, 11*(4), 515–528.

Wray, S. (2001). *The impact of using teaching portfolios on student teachers' professional development.* Paper presented at the American Educational Research Association Annual Meeting, Seattle, WA.

Wright, V. H., Stallworth, B. J., & Ray, B. (2002). Challenges of electronic portfolios: Student perceptions and experiences. *Journal of Technology and Teacher Education, 10*, 49–62.

Zidon, M. (1996, Spring). Portfolios in preservice teacher education: What the students say. *Action in Teacher Education, 18*(1), 59–70.

CHAPTER 1

TEACHER'S SELF-ASSESSMENT OF REFLECTION SKILLS AS AN OUTCOME OF E-FOLIOS

Robert J. Beck
Sharon L. Bear
University of California, Irvine

OVERVIEW

In this chapter, we propose that reflection skills are the most important objective of preservice teachers' portfolio investigations, and we present a method for assessing teachers' reflection skills as an outcome of their e-folios. A model of reflection was developed, based on Schon's (1983) concepts of reflection-on-action and reflection-in-action, coupled with Killion and Todnem's (1991) reflection-for-action. The model was researched as part of a "Preparing Tomorrow's Teachers to Use Technology" (PT3) grant that involved preparing teachers to use technology in creating e-folios. The model includes five dimensions of reflection: (a) general reflective skill, (b) assessment reflection, (c) reflections linking assessment and planning, (d) reflections on student work, and (e) collaborative reflection. Two types of portfolios were investigated: accountability portfolios, which serve licensure requirements and offer evidence of teachers' knowledge of standards

Evaluating Electronic Portfolios in Teacher Education, pages 1–22
Copyright © 2009 by Information Age Publishing

and pedagogy, and formative portfolios, which serve primarily to contribute to teachers' acquisition of reflection skills.

We hypothesized that preservice teachers would rate formative portfolios more highly with respect to reflection skills. In the research design, we compared four e-folio curricula, all of which used preservice teachers' case studies of academically challenged students as a method for supporting professional development. Three e-folios were formative, with teacher development as a primary objective, and used participants' narrative reflections on their students over a two- to three-month period. One e-folio was summative, assessing teacher accountability through preservice teachers' analyses of professional teaching standards relating to students, during one- to two-week teaching units. The reflective outcome dimensions were measured through a 34-item electronic Portfolio Assessment Scale (ePAS), in which teachers rated the development of their reflection skills after completing electronic portfolios. The results of the study showed that, as hypothesized, formative e-folios were rated as superior to summative, in terms of general reflective skill supporting teacher development, improved assessment role competencies, greater understanding of connections between assessment and planning, and relatively high value placed on teacher peer collaboration. However, the type of e-folio made no difference on self-reported benefits of analyzing student work. From this research, we developed a model of e-folios based on reflective inquiry as the most effective teacher development strategy associated with the learning of reflection skills. The chapter concludes with implications for the design of e-folio instructions and activities.

REFLECTION IN THE TEACHING CYCLE

Dewey (1933) referred to the bi-temporal character of reflection, citing both its retrospective and anticipatory modes, and stated that inquiry includes the "habit of reviewing previous facts and ideas relating them to one another on a new basis, namely, that of the conclusion that has been reached" (p. 118). Retrospective reflection is a hallmark of e-folios, in which teachers integrate their memories of classroom experiences and of particular students with facts and ideas, such as student work and pedagogical theories. These retrospective reflections are the basis for the revision of instruction. Additionally, prospective reflection is important in designing solutions, as Dewey explained: "Again it has been suggested that reflective thinking involves a look into the future, a forecast, or anticipation, or a prediction...while the final solution gives a definite set toward the future" (p. 117). From this perspective, reflection for future action is a way of attending to or framing a situation in anticipation of its occurrence. Anticipatory reflection potentially enables teachers to consider alternatives, develop new lesson plans, and anticipate the learning outcomes of students. Thus, Dewey believes that reflection consists both of the retrospective analysis of data and the prospective application of reflection to future plans.

A process of teaching practice, commonly addressed by e-folios, involves both retrospective and anticipatory reflection during what has been called the continuous improvement cycle of planning, instruction, and assessment. In the teaching cycle, a teacher's plans get implemented as instruction and undergo self-assessment and other formal assessments so that ineffective practices, usually, but also effective practices, deliberately become lessons learned. Lessons learned, in turn, are critically incorporated into new lesson plans, new instruction, and so forth. Reflection about connections between information obtained in their various roles and settings becomes useful in ensuring that the lessons learned become new lessons planned and innovations implemented. Therefore, reflections during the teaching cycle potentially constitute an inquiry involving interactions between plans, performances, and assessments, as well as making adjustments to plans, which then triggers a new cycle of experimentation and assessment.

The basis for the continuous improvement teaching cycle can be understood through Schon's (1983) concepts of reflection-on-action and reflection-in-action, coupled with Killion and Todnem's (1991) reflection-for-action. In reflection-on-action, teachers pause after an activity to reflect on how well it went. Such reflection can occur immediately following a learning activity, at the end of a school day or even at the end of a school term. Reflection-in-action is a more immediate process, in which teachers reflect in the midst of action. Such reflection involves an interweaving of thinking and action that enables teachers to grasp, in the moment, a problematic situation and to more or less immediately change their behaviors to better deal with the situation. Finally, reflection-for-action involves thought, then action. Such thought, derived from reflection *on* and *in* action, is used for the planning of future action.

If we return to the aspects of the teaching cycle, we can see these three types of reflection (*on, in,* and *for* action) at work. A teacher's plans (reflection *for* action) get implemented as instruction and undergoes self-assessment (reflection *in* action) so that both effective and ineffective practices become lessons learned (reflection *on* action). These are critically incorporated into new lesson plans and new instruction (reflection *for* action) and, in principle, the process continues cyclically. Grossman and Shulman (1994) explained this cycle as akin to the processes of pedagogical reasoning, stating that teachers use reflection for action for curriculum analysis and planning, reflection in action during instruction, and reflection on both action and thought when they evaluate their practice.

Therefore, it is theorized that reflections that occur as part of the teaching cycle, in both retrospective and prospective modes, strengthen particular roles of practice, such as assessment, as well as enable teachers to acquire the habit of mind for making connections between assessment and lesson planning. We believe that the use of student data, while reinforcing a general tendency for teachers to develop assessment-based instruction, also contributes to making connections between assessment and planning. Based largely on theoretical grounds, but also on an increasing number of empirical studies, we concluded that collaborative reflection during e-folio construction is a necessary support for individual reflective development. Thus, we posited five dimensions of reflection—general reflective skill, assessment reflection, reflections linking assessment and planning, reflections on student work, and collaborative reflection—each of which is discussed below.

General Reflective Skill

General reflective skill, as well as the other four dimensions of reflection listed above, is proposed to be an outcome of portfolio making. The improvement in reflective skills is frequently cited as a major benefit of portfolio making. Anderson and DeMeulle (1998) characterized the portfolio as enabling preservice teachers to become "reflective practitioners," while Freeman (1998) cited "increased reflection" as an outcome. McKinney (1998) noted the benefit of a "reflective stance," in which preservice teachers revisit and revise their ideas over time. Snyder, Lippincott, and Bower (1988) stated, "if we provide opportunities for thoughtful practice, our students would generate equally appropriate, generally consistent, higher caliber, more personally valuable 'standards' of their own" (p. 128). Finally, Tucker, Stronge, and Gareis (2002) discussed the role of portfolios, which they saw as a "tool for self-reflection," evaluation, and professional development. While the literature is in agreement that reflection, in general, is an outcome of e-folios, the types of reflection have not been specified.

It has been theorized that general reflective skill consists of competencies in making conceptual connections between the primary role functions of teaching—planning, instruction, and assessment. In the portfolios of this study, the preservice teachers reflected both on their historical relationships with individual students and on daily and weekly cycles of teaching with whole classes. In both spheres of reflection, they made assessments of their ability to meet the challenges of being a teacher and whether this reflective activity improved their understanding of students. We believed that, were these changes in teachers' understandings of teaching and learning significant, they would be associated with both improvements in their practice and in their abilities to reflect. In turn, improvements in ability to reflect would be associated with improved pedagogy and observational skills in the classroom.

Assessment Reflection

Preparing teachers to continuously monitor and assess instruction in their classrooms is a mandated objective of all teacher preparation programs in the state of California[1] (this is also an NCATE requirement), and assessment is generally considered the principal work of the portfolio. There is an increasing emphasis on the teacher's role as an assessor or evaluator, in which student outcomes are used to draw conclusions both about student learning issues and curricular effectiveness. The teacher as assessor operates according to scientific principles and understands that evidence of performance must be collected and analyzed according to an appropriate model or conceptual framework and conclusions drawn about the teaching and learning process.

The portfolios we studied were conceived primarily as a means of obtaining records of teachers' reflections-in-action and reflections-on-action. During portfolio making, to encourage thinking like an assessor, teachers were asked to write classroom narratives in which they described their teaching, as they performed continuous assessments in their classrooms and used the information to plan future instruction. The resulting narratives provided records by which teachers could be assessed both qualitatively and quantitatively on the comprehensiveness of their assessment behaviors in sample classrooms.

Assessment reflection-in-action can be seen when a teacher has just finished a class presentation or made a seatwork assignment. He or she then circulates throughout the classroom, assessing the follow-through performance of the prior instruction. At this time, the teacher may stop and talk with small groups and individuals in need of specialized scaffolding. There is ample opportunity in this context for the teacher to hold "reflective conversations" and receive "backtalk" from the environment (Schon, 1983). These instructional reflections may be largely generated by interactions with different students and groups, in which feedback stimulates new ways of looking at (reframing) a problem and can result in immediate adjustments in instruction. Reflection-on-action occurs when reflections that are drawn from in-class adjustments are combined with deliberate reflection, in which teachers apply what they have learned both to the planning of future instruction and to assessments to measure the effect of instruction.

Therefore, the assessment dimension of reflection is central. Through assessment, teachers can meet the multiple challenges of teaching. They accomplish this, primarily, by using assessments as the basis for improving their plans for instruction, which take individual student needs into account.

Reflections Linking Assessment and Planning: Backwards Planning

Wiggins and McTighe (1998) formulated a theory of "backwards planning" that advocated a planning process for instruction that begins at the end with goals or standards for teacher learning or understanding and "then derives the curriculum from the evidence of learning (performances) called for by the standard and the teaching needed to equip students to perform" (p. 8). This form of planning involves reflections that link assessment and planning, as well as looking both backwards and forwards when planning curriculum.

Backwards planning was a pervasive instructional objective in the teacher preparation program under investigation in the present study. Teachers were taught to use the three stages of backwards design: (a) identify desired results, (b) determine acceptable evidence, and (c) plan learning experiences and instruction. This third stage, which is based on the decisions made in the first two stages, moves the teaching cycle into the process of future planning. It is argued that backwards planning, therefore, contributes to aspects of reflection involved in the continuous cycle of reflective thinking, planning, and assessment. Methodologically, the use of backwards planning as a major component of teacher preparation raised some problems with the measurement of reflection as an outcome of the e-folio, as students may have developed such skills prior to portfolio construction. Because of this potentially confounding variable, we relied on differences between the types of portfolios to partial out the effects of portfolios versus the general effects of teacher preparation.

Reflections on Student Work

Lampert and Ball (1998) believe that learning how to ask and pursue questions is central to becoming a good teacher. When preservice teachers pose questions to themselves about student work, for which they must develop an answer, they are engaging in a form of reflective practice about such work. When reflecting on their teaching and its outcomes, Lambert and Ball recommended that teachers use multiple records of practice as artifacts, including journals, structured field notes, conversational transcripts, and student work. They view such artifacts as serving "both as records of what occurred and as representations of what one *does* in the course of [teaching]" (p. 52). Additionally, when these records are placed in multimedia databases, they afford the opportunity for multiple reflections and interpretations of events, drawing from the different kinds of evidence. They explained that, as teachers return to and reexamine their interpretations of records in the multimedia environment, using different sources of information, they are provided with an opportunity to get to know a student more deeply.

Finally, Lampert and Ball (1998) provided guidelines, which we believe are applicable to reflecting on student work, for posing and pursuing questions during e-folio construction:

- Identify and articulate a starting point for your investigation.
- Think about what you are curious about and interested in.
- Create a collection of items or evidence as you pursue your question.
- Drawing from video, [student] notebooks, and teacher journals, collect items that are relevant to your question or focus.
- As your collection grows, keep taking stock of what you are finding.
- Begin to make decisions about which items you want to include and how to best group the items you have collected.
- Write an analysis of what your collection suggests about your original question.
- Formulate your tentative findings.
- Appraise your work [about the student's work].
- [Write] a reflection on [the student's work]. (pp. 211–212)

While the analysis of student work may be considered a theoretically distinctive reflective activity, it also can be viewed as part of student assessment and, as such, may be confounded with the dimension of assessment reflection. Again, it is proposed to test whether the analysis of student work is a distinctive dimension of reflection by comparing the performance of different types of e-folios.

Collaborative Reflection

The concept of collaborative reflection is based on Schon's (1983) notion that reflective practice takes the form of a "reflective conversation with the situation" (p. 295). In such a "conversation with a situation," reflective practitioners function as agents, shaping the situation and making themselves a part of it. In the case of preservice teachers engaged in collaborative reflection during e-folio making, this reflective conversation takes place not with a situation directly, but with instructors and peers concerning reported situations. Nevertheless, the same principle applies—teachers who are engaged in a reflective conversation contribute to their colleague's shaping and understanding of the situation and, perhaps, to improving their reflective skills.

Feldman (1997) explained the value of the collaborative reflection process among teachers:

> They [teachers] begin with a cooperative process in which some of the teachers start to talk and the others listen. As they listen, they think about what is being said and relate it to their own histories, their intentions, and their relations to others. Reflection occurs, and the ones who have listened, respond. The responses are answers to questions, related anecdotes or bits of narrative, or questions, which act in the evolution of the conversants' direction. (p. 11)

Mishler (1990, 1995) stated that the hypothesized practices or theories made by the practitioner in inquiry-based research, such as case studies, need to take place in a community of practice. Such a community validates the trustworthiness of the claims from the vantage point of other practitioners. Theoretically, collaborative reflection, similar to reflections on student work, is a distinctive reflective dimension. Yet, like student work, it also can be viewed as part of the self- and student assessment process.

The challenge in measuring reflection is that, as conceptualized above, reflection consists of a variety of dimensions, including those concerned with the teacher's growth and student assessment and change, as well as metacognitive dimensions, that is, self-assessed changes in reflection skill. Although reflections on assessment, planning, and instruction are easily conceptualized as relatively independent dimensions, they also can be understood as interrelated. Certainly, backwards planning consists of both planning and assessment. As such, analysis of student work also can be considered part of assessment. Collaborative reflection, in which mentors and peers offer critiques of e-folio entries, is another form of assessment or meta-assessment. Because of the interrelatedness of all these dimensions of reflection, one purpose of our study was to establish the construct validity of these dimensions as independent. A second objective was to measure the strength of each reflective dimension as an outcome of portfolio condition, that is, formative versus summative.

ELECTRONIC PORTFOLIO ASSESSMENT SCALE (EPAS)

Based on the foregoing model, the ePAS was developed both to measure the five dimensions of reflection and assess the effects of the e-folios on professional development. The ePAS consisted of 34 self-report statements, of which 17 were positively phrased statements and 17 were negatively phrased statements about various effects of e-folio making, such as self-discovery, increased understanding of reflective practice, greater knowledge of students, backwards planning, better understanding of the role of assessment in planning and instruction, and support for the value of collaboration. Each item was scored on a 5-point Likert-type scale, ranging from 1 = "disagree very much" to 5 = "agree very much." The internal consistency of the scale was .92. In 2002, the ePAS consisted of only 31 items (a few negative statements were not included). The internal consistency of this 31-item scale was .91. A discussion of each of the five reflective skills and examples of related items are presented below.

General reflective skill included such outcomes as "better understand my challenges as a teacher," "will help me to improve my future practice," "better understand how to reflect on practice," and "led to self-discovery as a teacher." This skill also included such statements as "have a better understanding of students as the major challenge I face," "learned a lot about the student who was the subject of my portfolio," "can better meet students' needs through planning lessons," and "am a better observer of classroom events." Examples of items included: "I think I am a better observer of classroom events." "I discovered things about myself as I wrote the case."

Assessment reflection included such concepts as "better understand the role of assessment in planning instruction," "understand the different assessment roles played by teachers," "improved my ability to consider and meet students' needs when I plan lessons," and "creating portfolio analyses about my classroom enabled me to better understand the challenges of being a teacher." Examples of items included: "I think I have improved my ability to consider and meet students' needs when I plan lessons." "I think I better understand the role of assessment in planning instruction."

Reflections linking planning and assessment included such statements as "backwards planning is a very useful strategy in designing instruction" and "thinking like an assessor enabled me to see useful patterns of events in my classroom." Examples of items included: "I think I have improved my ability to consider and meet students' needs when I plan lessons." "The idea of 'thinking like an assessor' enabled me to see useful patterns of events in my classroom."

Reflections on student work included such concepts as "analyzing examples of student work can be of much help in understanding students." An example of an item for this dimension was: "I think that analyzing examples of student work can be of help in understanding students."

Collaborative reflection included such notions as "reading the case answers from other classmates via email is helpful," "giving and getting constructive feedback about the case answers via email is helpful," and "discussing case responses in small groups during class is helpful." Examples of items included: "I think that reading the case answers from other classmates via email might be helpful." "I think that giving and getting constructive feedback about the case answers via email might be helpful."

With this understanding of the five dimensions of reflection, we now have a basis for comparing the two main types of portfolios—teacher accountability (summative) and teacher development (formative)—in regard to the extent to which they engage these dimensions of reflection and, in turn, lead to certain beneficial outcomes. Our main concern, in undertaking this comparison, was to determine which type of portfolio had a stronger impact on teachers' self-assessment of benefits to their professional development in terms of different kinds of reflective understandings.

TWO TYPES OF PORTFOLIOS: TEACHER ACCOUNTABILITY VERSUS TEACHER DEVELOPMENT

A critical dilemma in designing portfolios for preservice and beginning teachers is whether the portfolio is primarily a vehicle for teacher licensing assessment or teacher development and whether these two objectives are compatible. On the one hand, from a teacher accountability perspective, several authors (Campbell, Melenzyer, Nettles, & Wyman, 2000; Klecker 2000; Wolf, Lichtenstein, & Stevenson, 1997) have advocated that the portfolio be used to evaluate the achievement of state content and performance standards. On the other hand, researchers such as Darling (2001) proposed that teacher development should take precedence and that narrative reflection is the best way to foster such development. Each of these types of portfolios is discussed below.

Summative Accountability Portfolios: California Teacher Performance Assessment Cases

The Teacher Performance Assessment (TPA) is a recent California summative accountability portfolio prototype (pact.gse.uci.edu/uci_tpa). Although the TPA was intended, in part, to promote teacher development, the largely summative assessment system was organized in response to increased demands of standards-based teacher accountability by the California legislature (SB 2042). The goal of the TPA is to demonstrate and ensure that teachers have fulfilled mandated standards of teaching and educational quality. The TPA requires that teachers show satisfactory performance in relation to state mandated Teacher Performance Expectations, which include making subject matter comprehensible to students, assessing student learning, engaging and supporting students in learning, planning instruction, creating and maintaining effective classroom environments, and developing as a professional educator. Many educators and legislators, who supported the TPA, viewed the portfolio as a method of accountability for these teaching standards. The instructions and prompts of the TPA portfolio referred only to making connections between planning, instruction, and assessment, according to different teaching standards, as part of the daily/weekly teaching cycle. Teachers also were encouraged to reflect on understandings achieved through this process in order to revise future practice, but only minimal guidance was offered on how to reflect.

Teacher Formative Development Portfolios: Narrative Cases

Darling (2001), who conducted one of the few empirical studies of portfolios, emphasized that preservice teacher development portfolios were most effective when they told coherent stories of their learning experiences. In her case study of 12 teachers performing a relatively open-ended personal and creative portfolio, she found that, if novice teachers were able to narrate coherent stories of their learning experiences, most could achieve personal growth and transformation in the process of becoming teachers. In fact, Darling had prompted them to think of the portfolio as a "narrative that tells a coherent story of your learning experiences in the program, and highlights thoughtful reflection on, and analysis of, these experiences ... it is an unfolding of your understandings about teaching and learning, and about your development as a professional" (p. 111). Darling's principal finding was that those students who were capable of narrating their experiences created successful, thematic portfolios. She explained, "making sense of one's experience and communicating it to others is a useful description of creating a narrative, especially when applied to building a portfolio ... emerging professional identities were documented, sometimes powerfully, through combinations of words and images ..." (pp. 119–120).

Students who wrote meaningful narratives of their experiences also expressed satisfaction with the portfolio as a learning experience about themselves and their students. However, some novice teachers were confused about what was required in the portfolio and experienced it as undefined and ambiguous. Some of these teachers wanted models of portfolios, at least to guide the early phases of instruction. As such, to assist novice teachers in creating a formative portfolio, detailed scaffolding may be needed. It is evident, as well, that Darling's limited sample requires that the assessment of narrative portfolios be conducted on a much larger scale.

Comparison between Formative and Summative Portfolios

The most important goal and process shared by both formative and summative portfolios is that they require teacher documentation of their thoughtful investigations of practice. In formative or teacher development portfolios, relatively long-term reflections predominate, while, in teacher accountability portfolios, relatively short-term standards-based analyses of the planning, instructing, and assessment teaching cycle are more central. Our main concern, in comparing the TPA with Darling's formative development oriented portfolio, was "Which type of portfolio has a stronger impact on teachers' self-assessment of benefits to their professional development?"

In undertaking this comparison, our position was that the promise of the portfolio consisted of fostering a powerful habit of mind, reflection, which would better enable teachers to make sense of and introduce effective change into their classrooms. We thus believed that portfolios relatively oriented to teacher development and that used narrative methods would better support teachers' positively evaluated outcomes than would a portfolio relatively oriented to the assessment of their understanding of professional standards. Although no published studies were found on sex differences in portfolios, we were curious as to whether females, as compared to males, might benefit more from a narrative approach to portfolio making.

PARTICIPANTS

The participants consisted of a total of 207 teachers, who were either in credential or Master of Arts in Teaching (MAT) programs at a research university or were beginning (one to two years) inservice teachers. There were four samples of preservice and inservice teachers drawn from MAT portfolio courses, taught by the first author, or credential program activities. Of the three samples of preservice teachers, one group, the Portfolio A sample, had 62 participants in an MAT course; another, the Portfolio B sample, had 67 preservice teacher participants in a credential program activity; a third, the Portfolio C sample, had 59 preservice teacher participants in an MAT course; and a fourth, the Portfolio D sample, consisted of 19 inservice teachers in an MAT course. Students in all portfolio programs created electronic case studies of K–12 students. They electronically submitted and stored a variety of descriptions and artifacts (e.g., plans, videos, student work) and wrote word-processed reflections on these data. After constructing one of the electronic e-folios described below, the ePAS was administered to these four groups of teachers.

PORTFOLIOS

Portfolio A

Portfolio A consisted of 21 questions that directed the construction of a formative teaching and assessment case. Teachers selected one or more lessons that they taught, for which they had collected samples of work from two students with "challenging learning characteristics." The case instructions called for teachers to write two different student biographic narratives and one comprehensive lesson narrative. Some questions prompted teachers to analyze how planning, teaching, and different assessment roles were used as part of the teaching cycle to improve their practice and know students better. Teachers interpreted artifacts as evidence to support their case analyses. During portfolio making, teachers collaborated by sharing their portfolios and received support from established teachers, including National Board Certified Teachers. While Portfolio A was primarily oriented to teacher development, it was considered a hybrid because it contained some summative assessment activities. Portfolio A was primarily concerned, therefore, with teacher development, understanding of assessment roles, understanding of backwards planning, the benefits of analyzing student work, and the value of teacher mentor and peer collaboration.

Portfolio B

The TPA summative portfolio directed teachers' analyses of a "teaching event," which is a teacher-selected connected series of lessons and related artifacts over a week or two. There were four areas of focus: instructional design, instructional performance, formal and informal assessment of student learning, and reflection on practice. The instructions asked novices to account for numerous aspects of their professional development. For example, the tasks for *instructional design* instructed the teacher to:

1. Select a series of lessons around a common concept, theme, or pedagogical goal.
2. Provide relevant information about students as learners of your subject matter and about expectations for student learning during the lessons.
3. Keep a daily log on the lessons and reflections on your instructions.

Other than in their analyses of teaching and learning, preservice teachers had little opportunity to reflect on discoveries they may have made that were not in specifically prescribed areas. Nevertheless, as an example of a summative accountability portfolio, the TPA is a well organized, comprehensive instructional activity that might have some benefits for teacher professional development, if these are not overshadowed by the myriad analytic exercises the process entails. Portfolio B was, therefore, primarily concerned with understanding of assessment roles, backwards planning, and the benefits of analyzing student work.

Portfolio C

This formative portfolio was based on Schon's (1983) model of reflective inquiry, with a relatively strong emphasis on metacognitive understanding and collaborative learning. Teachers were instructed that the reflective inquiry should be a story about their interactions with a student who had learning challenges and should tell about the transformation of their beliefs about this student and changes in the student's performance or explain why performance was still inadequate. Teachers also developed an experimental inquiry that described the evolution of their thinking about factors that might have contributed to the student's problem and the transformation of their instructional approaches with the student. The inquiry included the development of questions and problems and their representations, hypothesis formation, testing interventions, collecting and analyzing data, and theory making. Finally, teachers were asked to assess the value of reflective inquiry for their problem solving. Portfolio C was, therefore, primarily concerned with teacher development, the benefit of analyzing student work, and the value of teacher peer collaboration.

Portfolio D

This formative portfolio also was based, in part, on Schon's (1983) model of reflective inquiry, with some modifications involving greater emphasis than Portfolio C on using evidence. In particular, this portfolio used analyses of teacher-student dialogue as evidence of instructional effectiveness. Based on Lampert and Ball's (1998) guidelines, teachers were asked to record dialogues with a student, analyze their teaching strategies, and evaluate the student's learning difficulties. They also were asked to propose what could be done to foster student growth. During portfolio making, teachers collaborated by sharing their portfolios and received support from experienced teachers. Questions were employed that encouraged teachers' metacognitive understanding of the value of the portfolio to future practice. Portfolio D was, therefore, primarily concerned with teacher development, understanding of assessment roles, understanding of backwards planning,

TABLE 1.1   The Four Portfolios: Expected Outcomes

Portfolio	Teacher development	Understanding of assessment roles	Understanding of backwards planning	Benefit of analyzing student work	Teacher–peer collaboration
A	✔	✔	✔	✔	✔
B		✔	✔	✔	
C	✔			✔	✔
D	✔			✔	✔

the benefit of analyzing student work, and the value of teacher peer collaboration.

In conclusion, all four portfolios involved the use of K–12 student case study data and teachers' demonstrations of their understanding of the interrelatedness of planning, teaching, and assessment of student work. Table 1.1 presents a summary comparison of the four e-folios in terms of their expected outcomes.

EXPECTED OUTCOMES

Based on the differences in the portfolios, we made five predictions regarding outcomes. First, because they employed narrative methods addressing the long-term relationship between the e-folio maker and a student, Portfolios A, C, and D would be associated with greater benefits to teacher development than would Portfolio B. Second, because they focused on the assessment of teaching standards to a greater degree, Portfolios A and B would be associated with better understanding of assessment roles than would Portfolios C and D. Third, because they focused on teaching standards linking assessment and planning to a greater degree, Portfolios A and B would be associated with better understanding of backwards planning than would Portfolios C and D. Fourth, because all portfolios focused on the analysis of student work, Portfolios A, B, C, and D would not differ in terms of being associated with better understanding of the benefits of using student work. Fifth, because Portfolios A, C, and D involved mentor and/or peer collaboration during portfolio making, they would lead to more perceived benefits of teacher collaboration than would Portfolio B, which did not employ any form of collaboration during e-folio construction. Although we made no predictions, we also were interested in determining whether there were sex differences in participants' self-assessment of the benefits associated with the construction of portfolios.

RESULTS

Factor Analysis of the ePAS

Based on the model of reflection and the expected differences among the portfolios presented above, the validity of the internal structure of the ePAS was investigated by means of an exploratory factor analysis (Beck, Livne, & Bear, 2005). For each portfolio independently, the analysis resulted in five factors: (a) teacher development, (b) understanding of assessment roles, (c) understanding of backwards planning, (d) the benefit of analyzing student work, and (e) the benefit of teacher peer collaboration, each of which was a distinct dimension of our model of reflection.

- Factor 1, corresponding to general reflective skill, consisted of 12 items that corresponded to overall teacher development and general reflective skill. These items referred to understanding the challenges of being a teacher and of understanding students. Some of these items also referred to the acquisition of reflective skill.
- Factor 2, corresponding to assessment reflection, consisted of four items concerning understanding of assessment roles and one item that referred to understanding the challenges of being a teacher.
- Factor 3, corresponding to reflection linking assessment and planning, consisted of four items that tapped teachers' understanding of backwards planning.
- Factor 4 contained three items related to the benefit of analyzing student work and one item that referred to understanding reflection on practice.
- Factor 5 contained five items corresponding to collaborative reflection, all of which concerned the benefit of teacher peer collaboration in constructing e-folios.

Thus, of the 31 test items, 28 items were represented by the five factors.

Because five components had been found for each of the four portfolio groups, the internal structure of the ePAS was further examined by means of an exploratory factor analysis on the *combined sample* of the four groups of teachers (N = 207). The same five factors identified in the independent groups also were found for the aggregate sample. Taken together, the findings supported a model of reflection consisting of five distinct components associated with the benefits of portfolio making. In subsequent analyses, we used only items that had high loadings (> .50).

Differences in the Factor Mean Scores

On the basis of the five factors presented above, factor scores were used to measure differences among the participants' self-assessments, yielding three main findings. First, there were significant differences among four of the five factors (overall teacher development, including reflective skill, understanding of assessment roles, understanding of backwards planning, and benefit of teacher peer collaboration) for the four portfolios. Second, no significant differences were found for the benefit of analyzing student work for the portfolios. Third, no significant differences were found between female and male teachers, by portfolio group.

Overall Benefits of Portfolios for Professional Development

To determine the overall benefits of each of the four portfolios on teachers' professional development, the differences in their total mean scores on the ePAS were examined by a one-way analysis of variance. The results indicated that there was a significant difference between each of the three means of Portfolios A, C, and D versus the mean of Portfolio B. Specifically, teachers rated each of the four portfolios favorably, with mean scores above the midpoint. However, Portfolios A, C, and D were rated significantly higher for overall contribution to their professional development.

Findings as Related to Expected Outcomes

Overall, there was a generally positive assessment of Portfolios A, C, and D, as they contributed to overall teacher development, backwards planning, and teacher peer collaboration in professional development. Surprisingly, Portfolios A and B did not contribute to a greater understanding of assessment roles than did Portfolios C and D. While Portfolios C and D did not emphasize this understanding of assessment roles, we concluded that their use of theory-based reflective inquiry may have contributed to their effects on professional development in this regard. Moreover, Portfolio B, despite focusing on connections between planning and assessment, had a significantly different lower mean score on backwards planning as a perceived benefit of portfolio construction. According to our results, Portfolio B, the accountability portfolio, fared the most poorly.

Additionally, no significant differences were found between male and female teachers concerning professional development on any of the portfolios or factors. This suggested that electronic portfolios might provide a useful technique to enhance teachers' development, irrespective of their sex, and that narrative methods were not especially useful to females, as had been suspected.

DISCUSSION

The ePAS, in successfully differentiating between the e-folios on the factors of teacher development, backwards planning, and collaboratively learning, as predicted, should be considered a promising e-folio assessment technique. The findings derived from the ePAS support the conclusion that teacher e-folio designs should incorporate formative strategies, such as reflective inquiry, individual student and lesson narratives, and professional and peer support. The summative accountability portfolio was not found to contribute to teachers' professional development as strongly as did other portfolios, except as supporting the analysis of student work in making assessments. Because the summative e-folio fared worst in relation to three different competitors, and given that the use of summative portfolios are also under attack on legal grounds, the conclusion that portfolios should not be used for summative accountability seems persuasive.

However, we were puzzled about the findings that, contrary to expectations, showed that Portfolios C and D contributed significantly more to teachers' *understanding of assessment roles* than did Portfolios A and B. We had predicted that, because Portfolios A and B had targeted assessment roles, they would have been rated as superior. It could be argued, however, that the reflective inquiry strategies used in Portfolios C and D provided teachers with an experimental approach in which assessment was used more or less continuously to appraise results of interventions in relations with students, as well as in curricular innovations. Further, Portfolios C and D provided more theoretical guidance when directing teachers to assess change in their own beliefs and encouraged the use of learning theories in understanding and assessing teacher-student interactions. Therefore, these portfolios addressed the objectives of overall teacher development, including self-discovery and reflection, which were not addressed in Portfolio B. We speculate that Portfolio A, in its hybrid approach, was less successful in developing teachers' understanding of assessment roles because, on the one hand, this portfolio contained some accountability tasks, but, on the other hand, lacked an overall reflective inquiry strategy.

We also wondered whether the reflective dimensions of assessment roles and backwards planning are distinct enough, insofar as they share similar (but not identical) items referring to backwards planning. The assessment roles dimension addresses both specific assessment and planning concerns as well as teacher development in general, as seen in the item, "better understand the challenges of being a teacher." The presence of this item suggests that the conceptual domain being measured includes considerations beyond planning and curriculum, a feature of Portfolios A, C, and D. In contrast, in Portfolio B, training in different assessment roles may have been more limited, as assessments were made about curriculum alone. The backwards planning dimension uses the specific labels of "backwards planning" and "thinking like an assessor," and these may refer to the more general constructs of the related activities of planning and assessment. Therefore, backwards planning probably does stand as a distinctive outcome dimension, independent of assessment.

Model of Professional Development Outcomes of Portfolios

The results also contribute to a model of professional development and reflection skills outcomes through portfolio making that might be understood by interpreting the possible relationships among the five dimensions. The following model, drawn from the items of the ePAS factors that students endorsed, proposes causal connections among the reflection dimensions and is written in the self-descriptive language of teachers' self-assessment of professional development. Following is the authors' interpretation of connections among the factors.

By making the portfolio, I understand better how to reflect on practice and this has led to self-discovery. The portfolio process was enhanced through collaborative activity in interactively exchanging portfolio information electronically or being able to read others' portfolios electronically. As a result, I have better understanding of my students as the major challenge I face. I learned a lot about the student who was the subject of my portfolio than I knew before. So, I can better meet students' needs through planning lessons. Additionally, I can better understand students because I am a better observer of classroom events. I also can better understand students by analyzing examples of student work.

Constructing the portfolio has led to an increase in my understanding of assessment in planning. I also understand different assessment roles better. As a result, I have an improved ability to meet students' needs when I plan. This view of planning is consistent with my belief in thinking like an assessor and doing backwards planning.

The foregoing statements become more complex propositions to be tested as an outcome of portfolio making. It is our intention to elaborate the ePAS in these directions by constructing additional items that explicitly reference causal connections between the reflective dimensions and measuring participants' levels of agreement with such statements.

IMPLICATIONS FOR THE DESIGN OF E-FOLIOS

The results of this study and the preceding model suggest that e-folios should be structured for preservice teachers as formative assessments that are oriented to improving professional practices and reflective skills. We believe that it would be useful to provide preservice teachers with an understanding of the five-factor framework prior to beginning work on the e-folio. This would enable them to conceptualize the dimensions of reflection as both separate and interrelated. Further, it is important to teach the act of reflection as a cognitive mode by which preservice teachers can connect planning, instruction, and assessment.

Preservice teachers also need to be supported in their understanding of reflection as a form of student assessment and self-assessment that links both backward to instruction and forward to lesson planning. They should understand that the construct of backwards planning is a useful analog for reflection on the teaching cycle. The inclusion of the interpretation of student work can be justified on the basis of theoretical models of e-folio work (Lampert & Ball, 1998) and is clearly needed for student and curricular assessment. The benefits of collaborative reflection also should be communicated to teachers using theoretical writings and integrated into the portfolio making in the form of instructions for strategies to share portfolios during the development process.

Formative e-folios, in which teachers reflect on both in-classroom encounters and long-term relationships with students, appears to stimulate the process of reflection. This approach provides practitioners with a method—narrative representations of teacher-student instructional interactions—that affords them a naturalistic reflective medium. This may be contrasted with the method of Portfolio B, which limited the scope of reflection to a relatively brief cross-section of classroom practice. Because formative e-folios involve an extended series of narrative reflections involving the continuous interaction of planning, instruction, and assessment in relation to particular students, teachers may track the development of both the student's achievements and problems, as well as the adaptive transformations of their own practice.

REFERENCES

Anderson, R. S., & DeMeulle, L. (1998, Winter). Portfolio use in twenty-four teacher education programs. *Teacher Education Quarterly, 23*–31.

Beck, R. J., Livne, N. L., & Bear, S. L. (2005). Teachers' self-assessment of the effects of formative and summative electronic portfolios on professional development. *European Journal of Teacher Education, 28*(3), 221–244.

Campbell, D. M., Melenzyer, B. J., Nettles, D. H., & Wyman, R. M. (2000). *Portfolio and performance assessment in teacher education.* Needham Heights, MA: Allyn & Bacon.

Darling, L. F. (2001). Portfolio as practice: The narratives of emerging teachers. *Teaching and Teacher Education, 17,* 107–121.

Dewey, J. (1933). *How we think: A restatement of the relation of reflective thinking to the educative process.* Boston: Henry Holt.

Feldman, A. (1997). *The role of conversation in collaborative action research.* Paper presented at the annual conference of the American Educational Research Association, Chicago, IL.

Freeman, J. J. (1998). *The teaching portfolio as a vehicle for professional growth.* Doctoral dissertation, University of New Hampshire.

Grossman, P., & Shulman, L. (1994). Knowing, believing, and the teaching of English. In T. Shanahan (Ed.), *Teachers thinking, teachers knowing: Reflections as literacy and language education* (pp. 3–22). Urbana, IL: National Council of Teachers of English.

Killion, J. M., & Todnem, G. R. (1991). A process for personal theory building. *Educational Leadership, 43*(6), 14–16.

Klecker, B. M. (2000). Content validity of preservice teacher portfolios in a standards-based program. *Journal of Instructional Psychology, 27*(1), 35–38.

Lampert, M., & Ball, D. (1998). *Teaching, multimedia and mathematics.* New York: Teachers College Press.

McKinney, M. (1998, Winter). Preservice teachers' electronic portfolios: Integrating technology, self-assessment, and reflection. *Teacher Education Quarterly,* 85–103.

Mishler, E. (1990). Validation in inquiry-guided research: The role of exemplars in narrative studies. *Harvard Educational Review, 60,* 415–442.

Mishler, E. (1995). Models of narrative analysis: A typology. *Journal of Narrative and Life History, 5*(2), 87–123.

Schon, D. A. (1983). *The reflective practitioner.* New York: Basic Books.

Snyder, J., Lippincott, A., & Bower, D. (1988). Portfolios in teacher education: Technical or transformational? In N. Lyons (Ed.), *With portfolio in hand: Validating the new teacher professionalism* (pp. 123–142). New York: Teachers College, Columbia University.

Tucker, P. D., Stronge, J. H., & Gareis, C. R. (2002). *Handbook on teacher portfolios for evaluation and professional development.* Larchmont, NY: Eye on Education.

Wiggins, B., & McTighe, J. (1998). *Understanding by design.* Alexandria, VA: ASCD.

Wolf, K., Lichtenstein, G., & Stevenson, C. (1997). Portfolios in teacher evaluation. In J. H. Stronge (Ed.), *Evaluating teachers: A guide to current thinking and best practice* (pp. 193–214). Thousand Oaks, CA: Corwin Press.

NOTES

1. See Standard 5.4 of California Standards for the Teaching Profession.

CHAPTER 2

DIRECT EVIDENCE AND THE CONTINUOUS EVOLUTION OF TEACHER PRACTICE

Arthur Recesso
Michael Hannafin
Feng Wang
Benjamin Deaton
Peter Rich
Craig Shepherd
University of Georgia

BACKGROUND

Portfolios have enabled a host of practitioners, ranging from preparing-through-developing teachers and their supervisors, to monitor and document progress in meeting standards through which their practices are assessed. Stakeholders—faculty, cooperating teachers, mentors, school leaders, and agencies that oversee teaching standards—utilize portfolios to document quality and progress. A key purpose of portfolio assessment is to "determine if achievement of outcomes has occurred" through the processes of completing a task in addition to the final product (Reeves & Okey, 1996, p. 196). The National Council for Accreditation of Teacher

Evaluating Electronic Portfolios in Teacher Education, pages 23–47
Copyright © 2009 by Information Age Publishing
23

Education (NCATE, 2003), for example, requires teacher preparation units to *document* performance during preparation through snapshots of performance in individual courses; the units, in turn, must document both progress and areas in need of improvement. The National Board for Professional Teaching Standards (NBPTS) uses portfolios, including video documentation of teaching practice, to certify teachers' proficiency in their particular teaching field. School systems are beginning to use portfolios to document teacher progress and personal growth, and to define professional learning needs. While each of these efforts demonstrates progress towards the use of evidence for improvement of practice, they are largely isolated and unsystematic rather than continuous or sustained. Few document progress across the teacher's professional development continuum. According to Reeves and Okey (1996), portfolio assessment occurs only when "the assessment's purpose is specified, guidelines for assembling a portfolio are clarified, and criteria and procedures for judging it are identified" (p. 194). Given appropriate methodologies combined with tools and opportunities to document and access evidence of instructional practices, teachers can both better plan their professional development and implement daily classroom practices.

PURPOSE

The purpose of this chapter is to introduce Evidential Reasoning & Decision Making (ERDM)—a methodology that employs a wide array of evidence of instructional practices and their effects along a professional development continuum. We present a conceptual framework for continuous professional development, describe the stages associated with implementing ERDM, introduce initial instantiation of methods as a Video Analysis Tool (VAT), discuss changes in practices among faculty, preparing teachers, mentors, and inservice teachers who implement ERDM, and describe its potential impact at different stages of professional development. Finally, we identify issues as well as prospects for implementing ERDM as a formative methodology for developing a portfolio of practices.

APPROACH

Evidential Reasoning & Decision Making: A Primer

Evidential Reasoning & Decision Making (ERDM) enables different stakeholders to examine evidence systematically to examine relationship between practices and goals, such as attaining NBPTS certification, improving student mathematics achievement, or mastering inquiry teaching methodologies. Practices are teaching enactments, that is, how teachers actually utilize various methods, artifacts and tools *in situ*. ERDM provides direct evidence of the link between practices and target goals, and the means through which progress can be documented, analyzed and assessed. While ERDM methodologies are applicable for different stakeholders and along their respective professional development continua, this chapter focuses on those concerned with the preparation and development of teachers.

The ERDM methodology enables stakeholders to identify specific practices that contribute to success or failure in a given teaching-learning setting. It enables more precise study of teaching-learning events within complex teaching environments, simultaneously reducing interference or "noise" from extraneous aspects while amplifying critical actions and consequences within the event. In effect, the methodology guides the strategic linking of cues that stimulate one's need to make decisions (e.g., low student performance on physical science concepts) to teaching practices (inquiry based instruction) where evidence (lesson plans, teacher work sample, video of instruction) can be collected and equated.

ERDM Framework

The ERDM process is summarized in Table 2.1.

Teacher Professional Continuum

As teachers evolve from initial preparation to induction and through their careers, their professional learning needs change; accordingly, the ERDM focus shifts. For purposes of this chapter, consider three phases of a teacher's career continuum: initial preparation, induction, and career professional.

Initial Preparation

The preparation of new teachers has been complicated by mandates to address an ever-broadening range of responsibilities, to document student accomplishments and progress, to guarantee compliance with certification and accreditation standards, and to support teachers as they develop initial competence. Typically, these efforts are compartmentalized in teacher preparation programs, addressing the letter, but often not the spirit, of the mandates. ERDM seeks to link, by design, evidence associated with these and related initial teacher preparation mandates with the practices presumed to cultivate them.

TABLE 2.1 ERDM Stages and Continuous Improvement

	Teacher professional continuum		
	Preparation	Induction	Career professional
Identifying triggers	Multiple areas to focus on. At this point focus on the values of domain for instructional practices. May use mock student data in methods or actual student data in field experiences and student teaching.	Refining knowledge about own practices, identifying areas of improvement, and addressing concepts of which students typically struggle. Utilizes performance data of students in grade level course.	Strategic selection of elements of practice that can be improved. Also thinking about successes that can be shared with others for their learning. Utilizes performance data of students in grade level course.
Marshalling evidence	May be from mockup or actual field experiences. Use evidence of practitioners in the field to clarify expectation and basis for comparison. Work with support professional to schedule when concepts are being addressed and/or strategies are being used.	Collected from multiple practitioners in domain or department. Expert guidance is provided by rater or support professional. Align to multiple days in syllabus and schedule of teaching concepts and use of broad instructional strategies. May be data driven or historical knowing the issues that challenge beginning teachers. May be aligned to phases of first year teacher.	More self-directed identification of evidence required to explain attributes of practices that can be changed for improvement. Align to specific lessons or sub-parts of lesson when teaching specific concepts and specific instructional strategies. May be aligned to phases of Career Professional teacher.
Interpreting evidence	Completed with rater or support professional using national, state, and preparation program standards.	Self and collaborative reflection engaging a distributed team using national, state, or school system standards.	Using national, state, or school system standards to continually refine practices as the issues at hand are more intricate. Improved communication of findings with raters and practitioners to inform their practices.
Developing course of action	Refine skills for defining critical elements and issues of practice. Trajectory of progress towards expected outcomes (e.g., standards) during preparation program.	Plan for improvement during school year with follow up each year. Trajectory of improvement at stages of career. Plans for refinement of action plan each year.	Increasingly focused on success to be shared with preparing and developing practitioners.

Evidential Reasoning & Decision Making

Throughout initial teacher preparation, prospective educators become increasingly aware of expectations defined by state and national certification and accreditation agencies as well as the standards advanced by professional organizations (NCATE, 2003; International Society for Technology in Education (ISTE), 2001; National Science Teachers Association (NSTA), 1998; National Council of Teachers of Mathematics (NCTM), 1998). Ironically, few preparing teachers know whether they are progressing toward such standards. Through portfolio-based ERDM, the initial performance of preservice teachers can be benchmarked using evidence. In addition, individual profiles of strengths and weaknesses can be established and updated based on evidence of progress, and used to compare practices with peer students or colleagues in the field.

Beginning teachers routinely indicate that the student teaching experience has the greatest impact on their initial preparation (see, for example, National Commission on Teacher and America's Future (NCTAF), 1996). Faculty supervisors and cooperating teachers guide and support student teachers through the experience. ERDM can strengthen the guidance provided as well as the quality of the experience by providing teacher educators and student teacher supervisors the means to document, and systematically address, the preservice teacher's emergence (or lack) of fluency along a wide range of competencies. For example, upon viewing a video sample of a secondary science preservice teacher, a faculty supervisor may recognize an instance where a specific NSTA standard is not being addressed. The ERDM methodology allows the supervisor to use specific teaching evidence and work in coordination with the student teacher to refine planning and methods for delivering that content.

ERDM can also help to mitigate the influence of distance and time, especially in rural areas where preservice teachers are routinely placed far from their supporting institution. Faculty supervisors typically travel great distances and thus are able to conduct only infrequent and limited observations; as a consequence, they often provide only minimal feedback to student teachers. With ERDM, preservice teachers can capture video samples of their teaching and upload the video and/or other evidence (lesson plans, student products, teaching materials, student performance data, etc.) for faculty review. Alternatively, live video of student teaching practices can be streamed, observed by the faculty supervisor, and assessed at a distance in real time. This capability mitigates the barrier of physical distance and increases both the number and flexibility of opportunities to observe preservice teacher practices.

Induction

The induction phase, typically the first three years of teaching, proves especially challenging for many new teachers, as the support and guidance provided during initial preparation often declines significantly. First-year teachers encounter particular challenges as they enter a new culture, adapt to new personalities, expectations and organizational norms, and often have only limited support beyond their immediate peers. For example, wide variability exists—both in the teaching domain and teacher facilitation expertise—among those who rate, evaluate or otherwise oversee teaching practices during induction. Relatively few administrative supervisors, for example, have significant mathematics or science expertise or are well-versed in the pedagogical practices advocated by national groups such as NCTM or NSTA. Yet, they routinely evaluate the practices of teachers in different domains, often relying on anecdotal data and broad, informal observation instruments rather than the values, methods and approaches advocated in those domains. As an unintended consequence, leaders and mentors, unintentionally but often systematically, can undermine the very pedagogical values and competencies their teachers strive to support.

Finally, induction teachers rarely have the opportunity to examine, systematically, their own teaching practices, or to gain the benefit of a local mentor's "critical eye" as to those practices. That is, while support is often available from more experienced peers, such support tends to be more socially than pedagogically based. Rarely do peer mentors analyze evidence of an induction teacher's actual teaching practices; when they do, the analysis tends to be holistic rather than "particular" in nature. Ideally, teaching practices should also be scrutinized by peer practitioners who have similar age-grade assignments, domain responsibilities and pedagogical values (e.g., inquiry questioning and probing by middle-school science teachers). In the face of limited or failed induction phase support, beginning teachers may tacitly acquiesce to misguided or misinformed local pressures or simply revert to teaching "how they were taught."

ERDM provides a means through which supervisors can broaden and deepen their understanding of teaching practices and values in different domains, and individual and collaborative assessment of teaching practices can be accomplished. Through ERDM, a range of "lenses" can be applied through which teaching practices can be identified systematically, captured, coded, and analyzed. Induction science teachers in poor, rural schools, for example, can document their specific teaching practices in specific units, such as posing open inquiry questions, as they solicit feedback from experienced peers as to the effectiveness of their questioning, degree of student engagement, and relevance to the lesson goals.

Career Professional

Post-induction Career Professional teachers evolve from competency building as a novice to professional educators and contributors to the field. Early career professionals seek opportunities for continued growth, having gained confidence and understanding in critical elements of classroom practice. The range of opportunities afforded these teachers to develop their own (and others') practices, however, varies greatly in quality and focus. Most teachers must rely on largely informal strategies for growth and improvement, and self-identified resources to support career enhancement. Few have an established career trajectory, with well-defined developmental milestones; fewer still have well-developed means to support either self- or peer improvement along such a continuum.

ERDM methods and tools provide a capacity to capture, analyze, and share effective practices. These methods and tools have become increasingly important in addressing existing standards and requirements for career improvement, such as attaining NBPTS recognition as well as the ability to support preservice and induction teachers' use of exemplary practices of accomplished teachers. Rather than solely providing a snapshot of video teaching practices for NBPTS consideration, for example, ERDM portfolios enable the documenting of emergent teaching practices over time, with evidence of continuous improvement over time of targeted methods and approaches. Simultaneously, ERDM enables the development of an indexed video library of specific teaching practices through which accomplished teachers can support beginning teachers by identifying critical teaching events and clarifying standards-based competencies as they occur (Hill, Hannafin, & Recesso, 2007). Evidence-based mentor training and support establishes a renewable repository of mentor-modeled strategies for the protégé to enact as he/she improves his/her own, and eventually others', practices.

ERDM Stages

ERDM guides stakeholders in how to elicit and use stage-appropriate evidence keyed to different phases of the continuum. As shown in Figure 2.1 and elaborated in Table 2.1, we focus on 4 stages: identifying triggers; marshalling evidence; interpreting evidence; and enacting a course of action.

Stage 1. Identifying Triggers

Triggers are cues or signals that serve as a precursor to identifying a specific practice or parts of practice within ERDM and the corresponding roles and responsibilities of those involved. In the context of continuous teacher professional development, triggers essentially cue one to "take notice" and become aware that a decision needs to be made, that is warranting further inquiry. Where key teacher activities presumed to be linked to specific performance indicators, outcomes or competencies, triggers signal the need for improvement or replication of success. In a 3rd grade math-

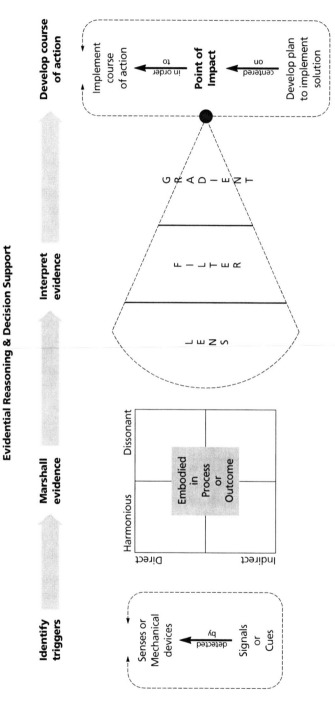

Figure 2.1 Stages of Evidential Reasoning & Decision Making.

ematics lesson focusing on using common fractions to represent parts of a whole, for example, a trigger might originate when a teacher implements a strategy presumed to improve student performance. The teacher's conceptual understanding of the link between fractions and visual representations becomes apparent during observation of practice. For teacher educators or teacher mentors, the trigger might be disparities between desired and expected pedagogical referents, such as those proffered by the NCTM for visualizing mathematics. Those assessing teacher practice establish an initial focus by aligning the trigger to a common framework of teaching practice standards (e.g., NCTM standards) and parameters for inquiring about practices during a very specific place and time.

The importance of focus is often difficult for preparing teachers to grasp. Preparing teachers often have a very broad conceptual understanding of practices and student learning, but little experience from which to examine or understand their meaning. Further, they do not readily view their specific practices as evidence of particular pedagogical values or techniques, nor do they tie such practices to common frameworks or particular student outcomes. They need assistance focusing on not only how to improve, but also on how to identify specific practices deemed consistent with teaching standards, motivation, or student achievement. During induction, teachers begin to refine their focus because they are increasingly aware of the nuances of specific instructional strategies and the ways in which students construct knowledge. Career Professional teachers are better able to use triggers to pinpoint both their strengths to be reinforced and their weaknesses to be improved; they are also increasingly capable of supporting one another in their career development, sharing triggers for their mutual benefit.

Stage 2. Marshalling Evidence

Marshalling evidence involves systematically connecting a focus to events. To marshal evidence, we begin to refine or further specify the evidence needed. Since recognition of multiple problems can prove overwhelming to preparing and induction teachers, mapping evidence to embody fine grain attributes of practice explicitly helps the novice to focus on important teaching-learning issues. Faculty and cooperating teachers assist the preparing teachers to define evidence known to capture representations of their instructional focus and identify when evidence of key practices will be available to be collected (e.g., when practices are enacted in the classroom). Induction teachers often receive assistance from a more experienced peer or school leader in ways to use evidence to refine the nuances of their methods. Career Professional teachers typically as well as student teachers and induction teachers in related domains model the use of evidence in professional improvement. That is, they know the value of looking at evidence that represents effective practice.

Evidence is embodied in teacher practice (e.g., lesson plans that guide the enactment, instructional materials used in conjunction with strategies, worksheets), student learning (e.g., work samples, questions generated), and leader decision making (e.g., memos, vision statement, building level assessment of teacher and learner performance). Evidence of student performance is typically found in independent assessments of comprehension or engagement, such as test scores and participation in discussion and group activities. Evidence of teaching as well as student performance, a cornerstone of ERDM in teacher professional development, can be obtained by videotaping classroom events as teachers enact strategies (or not) and learners engage (or not). In ERDM, we systematically link evidence in the form of artifacts, tools, and measures with student and/or teacher criterion measures to interpret and inform practices.

Evidence of practice is used iteratively as teachers' progress from initial preparation through Career Professional. Preparing teachers initially examine their existing evidence to better understand how accomplished practices, those that address national and state standards, are enacted by experienced teachers. Methods courses provide opportunities to learn and practice different approaches, while student teaching provides opportunities for prospective teachers to collect initial evidence of their own practices, essentially benchmarking individual practices to be refined throughout their career. With the sustained support of both teacher education program faculty and local peer support, induction teachers build on their initial experience, documenting evidence of their practices and continually re-referencing other evidence related to their practices. Career Professional teachers seek to fine-tune both their teaching practices and the precision with which they gather and use direct and indirect teaching and student evidence.

Stage 3. Interpreting Evidence

The interpretation stage is designed to specify areas to be reinforced or improved based upon a clear association between activities and evidence corroborating or questioning the effectiveness of those activities. Frameworks, or lenses, establish the parameters and criteria by which performance will be examined. Frameworks define the indicators through which practices can be examined, and in some cases, how far a teacher has evolved along the professional continuum. Typically, the framework employs rubrics designed to codify the extent to which performances can be differentiated qualitatively. For example, International Society for Technology in Education (ISTE) and NCATE standards might be used to analyze evidence of the technology integration practices of preparing teachers to assess the extent to which they approach, meet, or exceed defined standards. Likewise, NSTA standards might be applied as a lens to gauge the extent to which science teachers demonstrate specific inquiry strategies in their teaching, or NCTM standards may be used as rubrics to examine how well teachers demonstrate mathematics visualization strategies in their instruction. Increasingly, interest has emerged in documenting the student performance consequences of standards-based practices.

Interpretation is critical to setting a trajectory for improvement as teachers document and monitor their professional growth. Preservice teachers practice their instructional strategies primarily with faculty and peers, providing a safe, simulated setting for initial teaching efforts. Evidence of their performance is typically limited to the professional judgment of the teacher educator, and the standards of practice appropriate to their field, but little authentic student performance evidence is available. Induction teachers, in contrast, refine their knowledge and skills in situ with the help of peers, as well as grade-level or department teams. Peer and supervisor ratings can be analyzed in conjunction with student performance evidence, increasing both the authenticity and the utility of analysis for improvement, to reflect individually or collaboratively, to clarify expectations, and to consider alternatives.

Stage 4. Developing a Course of Action

A course of action is a plan to improve or modify practices or artifacts attributed to successful or unsuccessful performance. Implementation of the course of action resumes at the trigger where the process was initiated, establishing an iterative system designed to improve both the quality of teaching practices and the outcomes of those practices.

As a process, ERDM enables teachers to establish and monitor a trajectory of progress across the professional development continuum based on the impact of their practices, not simply certificates earned or courses completed. Preservice teachers identify initial perspectives and approaches that are deployed during student teaching, and refined using rater evidence specific to the values and priorities of their teacher education program. During induction, they refine both beliefs and practices using both increasingly authentic student and teaching evidence, and the support of their school teams. Career teachers can continue to fine-tune and expand their repertoire, as well as to capture their experience, knowledge, and skills for the benefit of the next-generation of teachers.

IMPLEMENTING ERDM

For simplicity, we describe two "classes" of ERDM stakeholders: practitioners and raters. Practitioners, in the present context, include those whose progress is measured or examined using ERDM tools and methods. In the present context, these include individual teachers or teams of teachers seeking to improve their performance (e.g., refining science inquiry questioning, raising test scores at a given grade level via precision teaching, improving classroom management, increasing student motivation), school leaders or teams of leaders interested in improving some aspect of performance (e.g., interaction with faculty, utility of evaluation methods, decision-making in resource allocations, etc), or other individuals or groups who share common goals, interest in assessing the impact of practices, and concern with improving the impact of practices. Raters include educators in the role of assessing the practices of other for the purposes of gauging progress and/ or supporting improvement. Raters assist practitioners by assessing their practices, providing both evidence as to the impact of practices and feedback as to possible improvements.

As depicted in Table 2.2, relationships between raters and practitioners can be formal or informal. One support professional rater, for example, may be a vice principal who provides formal quarterly evaluations of a teacher's performance; these ratings often are conducted for summative purposes, such as annual performance reviews. The assistant principal's observations can also be formative, such as identifying the teacher's use of examples from everyday living, in order to recommend an immediate or long-term supportive course of action. In contrast, teachers may apply ERDM methodology to provide feedback about the support offered by a more experienced peer through periodic evaluation of a mentoring program. The teacher and mentor might maintain a log of their discussions and interactions to document changes and improvements that result from analyzing video evidence of classroom practices. Informally as both rater and teacher, for instance, a science department head may study student work samples and lesson plan evidence to identify the impact of a beginning teacher's approaches to teaching ecosystems. ERDM methods and tools provide flexibility to support the varied formal and informal roles and responsibilities of both teachers and support professionals.

Evidential Reasoning & Decision Making in Practice: Video Analysis Tool

ERDM systems guide decision-making practices, reifying a focus on instructional improvement, and enabling individual and collaborative reflection and feedback. The Video Analysis Tool (VAT), developed and refined through funding by the U.S. Department of Education Preparing Tomorrow's Teachers to use Technology (PT3), will be used to demonstrate how raters and practitioners engage in the ERDM methodology and portfolio development for continuous improvement, support and monitoring of

TABLE 2.2 Interaction and Interrelationships Between Rater and Practitioner

		Rater			
		Teacher		Support professional	
		Formal	Informal	Formal	Informal
Practitioner	Teacher	Mentoring program for induction teachers uses direct evidence with reciprocal mentoring strategies. Mentor and protégé collaboratively analyze anchored videos and reflect on beginning teacher's implementation of strategies.	Ad-hoc discussion about attending a professional learning opportunity based on recent analysis and course of action defined to improve practices.	Evidence collection and analysis of evidence using national teaching standards leads to recommended course of action as a professional development plan.	Student teacher adapts approach to teaching content after discussing strategies with university Arts & Sciences professor.
	Support professional	Career professional teachers provide feedback to school leader about observation methods and course of action leading to professional learning opportunity and support.	Teachers talk with school leaders about opportunities to disseminate successful implementation of new innovations in their classroom to teachers in other buildings.	System level leadership will implement a distributed model of leadership in the school building whereas the vice principal will be facilitator of a team to evaluate teacher practices.	Using direct evidence as an impetus for brainstorming about improving faculty and cooperating teacher roles and relationships with student teachers and impact on student learning.

teaching practices. The system's theoretical framework is adapted from Hannafin, Hill and McCarthy's (2002) four-component model for facilitating performance of ill-structured tasks, featuring contexts, tools, and resources.

Contexts—imposed, induced, or user-defined—establish the circumstances and conditions under which VAT uses and practices will vary. Imposed contexts are usually specific problems to be solved or issues to be resolved by either raters or practitioners. Imposed contexts can range from situations posed to determine how one might address a prototypical problem to actual events that unfold dynamically, unpredictably, and in real-time. A supervising teacher, for example, might ask a student teacher to enact specific pedagogical approaches as her fourth graders attempt to solve mathematics problems. Alternatively, a vice principal might encounter a physical confrontation between rival high school students, and need to apply Board-mandated procedures to address the situation. In each instance, the skills or capacity to enact specific practices would be considered sufficiently important as to warrant evidence that the appropriate skills have been demonstrated. Imposed contexts tend to be employed mainly during initial rater and practitioner development, as they acquire initial competence in the knowledge and skills associated with their respective roles.

Induced contexts, in contrast, typically elicit rather than prescribe situations to be addressed; again, induced contexts range from hypothetical (but plausible) to actual situations for which no clear or specific approach is considered "ideal" or required. For example, a supervising teacher might introduce a classroom scenario where several children are unruly and disruptive; the student teacher's task might be to identify the problem and suggest or implement alternative procedures to establish better classroom control. The majority of professional practitioners' effort occurs in authentic, induced contexts, where they flexibly adapt to circumstances for which no absolute or specific approaches are appropriate. Experienced practitioners and raters routinely alter their approaches, drawing on a wealth of knowledge and experience as they recognize teachable moments, deal with unforeseen circumstances, and otherwise flexibly adapt as situations dictate. Induced contexts are most appropriate to experienced raters and practitioners who have acquired more advanced expertise in their craft.

User-defined contexts address the individual goals and needs of different raters and practitioners, such as a high school science teacher seeking to refine open-inquiry questioning methods per NBTS guidelines or the vice principal seeking to become informed as to the pedagogical values of the science community. Different user-defined contexts, in effect, stimulate different ERDM applications for both raters and practitioners. User-defined contexts are generally most appropriate for career professionals, where advanced competency has already been demonstrated and greater emphasis on individual rather than institutional goals for improvement become prominent.

Tools provide the means to conduct inquiries, locate key information, mark-up video representations of practices, and otherwise manipulate evidence and communicate findings and recommendations for improvement. Ongoing collaborations with teacher educators, preservice teachers, and inservice teachers has resulted in several ERDM-specific tools, ranging from those that enable users to locate specific coded practices, apply meta-data tags to video events, as well as to capture, code, and analyze practices. The revised VAT system provides four kinds of tools: coding, processing, manipulation, and communication tools. Coding tools, such as VAT's included standards alignment, help users to tag desired information effectively and efficiently. Processing tools enable VAT users to gather and structure resources, such as uploading and data export tools. Communication tools are used to share information among raters and practitioners, including online messaging tools, discussion boards, and listserv servers. ERDM annotations, for example, both add information to existing evidence and help practitioners locate task or function-specific evidence more easily and effectively (Recker, Walker, & Lawless, 2003; Recker & Wiley, 2001).

A coding agent provides a means through which raters and practitioners can manipulate, test, and refine their knowledge and practice per user-specific criteria. For example, after the initial "analysis" stage, a student teacher's technology integration evidence may be rated informally by a supervising teacher or teacher educator according to Levels of Technology Integration (LoTI) standards (see http://www.loticonnection.com/whatisloti.html), using rubric-assigned values or differential quality based on their technology integration efforts. During the "develop a course of action" phase, student teachers may modify specific sections of the lesson plan, review the plan per items and quality indicators of the corresponding standards, and predict a change or improvement score to anticipate the effects of their changes.

Finally, *resources* comprise assets and data considered important to understanding, evaluating, or improving teaching practices. Each individual teacher amasses a variety of both teacher and learner centered evidence related to his or her specific teaching approaches, while also gaining access to evidence from other teachers, such as exemplary practices, inquiry libraries of various teaching approaches, and suggestions for development. Resources stored in the system are dynamic in that they can be changed by their providers if necessary. Moreover, users can comment and share their comments with other users. In this regard, their comments become new resources helpful for future use and improvement of the existing assets as well as developing other useful information.

TABLE 2.3 Performance Support Characteristics of the VAT System

Feature	Description	Instantiation in VAT
Contexts: Circumstances that define how tool use is situated		
Imposed	External agent	Topics to be focused on or problems to be solved as required by raters
Induced	Real or virtual	Existing or conceptual inquiries helpful for practitioners to find their learning or performance topics
User-defined	Individual determines what problem and/or need to address	Learning or performance needs identified by practitioners
Tools: Means for locating, accessing, and manipulating resources		
Searching	Locating specific resources	Keyword search; visual knowledge maps; inquiry library
Processing	Gathering and structuring information, analyzing resources or data	Video capture and upload; resources or scaffolds upload and organizing; creating, refining, and defining video clips; online notebook; portfolio publication
Manipulating	Testing and refining resources, examining or modifying contents	The ERDM assessment agent
Communicating	Sharing information or clarifying meaning	Online messaging; discussion board; listserv
Resources: Information available to or represented within the system		
Static	Stable, contents do not change	Video inquiries published by users.
Dynamic	Contents change through use	Existing resources can be changed by their providers. Users comment existing resources and share their comments.

VIDEO ANALYSIS TOOL: COMPONENTS & FUNCTIONS

The Video Analysis Tool (VAT) provides video capture and analysis tools for defining and reflecting on evidence of practices (See http://vat.uga.edu for more complete descriptions and samples of the capture and coding technology). Teaching-learning practices are recorded through video cameras and stored into the VAT server for review or analysis. Video evidence can be captured in two forms: live, real-time capture and post-event upload. In live capture, an IP video camera is pre-installed in a classroom, passing video streams to a video server which records the video streams, enabling a rater to observe practices unobtrusively with minimal classroom disruption or interference. Post-event upload refers to archiving video files on the

VAT server subsequent to recording a practice. VAT users can videotape an event in real-time, and subsequently digitize and upload the converted files to the server. While increasing the time and effort required to gather evidence, post-event uploading provides additional backup in the event of network or data transfer failures, as the local IP camera can also store the video files locally to be uploaded afterwards.

Video analysis enables raters and practitioners to conduct deep inquiries into teaching-learning practices. They can view a video of specific events and segment the video into smaller sessions of specific interest keyed to defined areas, needs or priorities. Refined sessions, called VAT clips, are especially useful in tightening the scope of an inquiry, providing both practitioners and raters the ability to observe and reflect without the "noise" or "interference" of extraneous events.

The rater accesses captured evidence of practice from a standard computer using Video Tools available through the VAT interface: refine clip, view my clips, and view other's clips. Through *refine clip* (Figure 2.2) two levels of coding can be completed, an initially large video segmenting of the overall video takes place, providing markers or reminders of where target practices might be examined more deeply. After initial live observation or during post-event review, the rater continues to use the *refine clip* function to make further passes at each segment to define specific, finer grained activi-

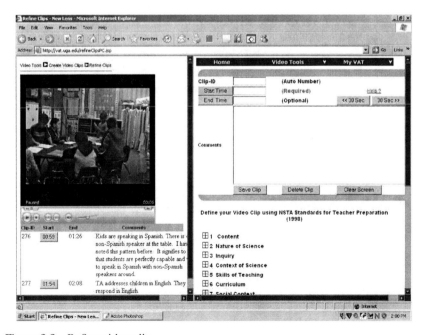

Figure 2.2 Refine video clip.

ties, such as when specific math teaching strategies occurred. During the refinement, the user defines clips where specific evidence is associated with criteria of interest, such as particular teaching frameworks, career benchmarks, or quality of practice rubrics. The user designates, annotates, and certifies specific events clips as representative evidence associated with a target practice, such as a national teaching standard (e.g., NBPTS standards). Marked-up, performance evidence can then be accessed and viewed for either a single individual or across practitioners using the *view my clips* function (Figure 2.3). This tool provides raters with the capability to examine closely the performance of a single individual across multiple events, or multiple individuals across single events. Finally, through the *view other's clips function* (Figure 2.4), users can share clips and reflections with raters or other practitioners, collaboratively reflecting and comparing their perspectives on and analysis of the events.

Users can also form groups through VAT. Practitioners grant and revoke the right to view each others' practices, providing the capacity, but not the requirement, to share evidence of their practices and ratings; groups, in turn, may also opt to restrict or share evidence of their member's practices. In the My VAT area, practitioners are able to edit their profile, upload files, modify file information, and assign markup or viewer rights (Figure 2.5) based on their preferences and the context of VAT use. Individual inquiry builders—practitioners or raters—may share evidence either face-face or asynchronously through a Web-based viewer interface. Members can view a

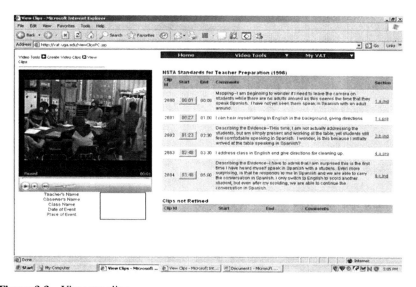

Figure 2.3   View my clips.

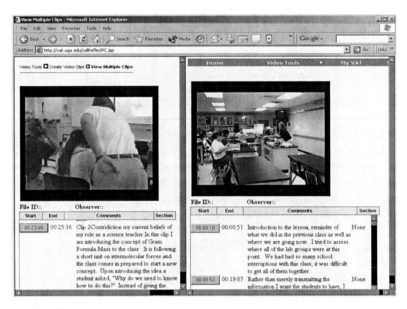

Figure 2.4 View others' clips.

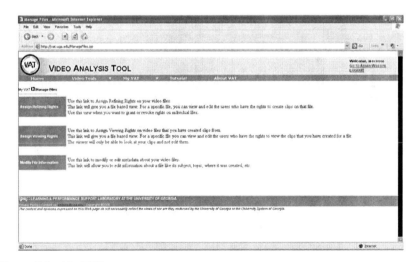

Figure 2.5 My VAT.

single piece of evidence, a complete inquiry, and even compare individual pieces (e.g., beginning and end of the semester) of evidence using the collaborative reflection tool. Through this interaction, the group sets a joint course of action or contemplates recommendations already tendered for the inquiry.

To assist users in fully utilizing functions of VAT, an online tutorial provides scaffolding in the form of step-by-step operation procedures as well as explanations of what each step means.

ERDM Stages & VAT: An Example

Preservice teachers, inservice teachers, school leaders, faculty, and mentors access the Toolkit as raters and/or practitioners through VAT's Web-based interface. Upon entering the site as group members and/or inquiry-builders within a group, users will encounter a current list of inquiries. Then, they are able to use existing functions to continue refining an existing inquiry or to build a new inquiry. For example, a district-level mathematics director, as rater, may define a focus by uploading video of students using Excel to construct their understanding or probability, accessing a lens helpful for analyzing the scores, and identifying a sub-domain problem as a priority, such as using the basic laws of probability a specific 8th grade mathematical concept.

The lens function used for associating standards with events, in turn, may clarify the context of teaching probability during the school year. During the face-to-face collaboratively using VAT the mathematics curriculum director (as rater) can schedule specific dates to observe 8th grade classes learning to find the probability of simple, independent events, for example, and plan to observe both teachers (as practitioners in this case) and students who excel or struggle with that concept. The rater is then prompted (scaffolded) to collect additional evidence such as past performance data, existing lesson plans and curriculum materials, and "proven effective" professional development practices related to the target priority need. The team of 8th grade mathematics teachers, including the mathematics curriculum director, then analyzes lesson plans, student work samples, instructional materials used to teach the concepts, and video segments of actual in-class teaching practices captured over two days where the target concept is introduced then applied. Subsequently, the team uploads and analyzes its evidence using NCTM and state learning standards and teaching rubrics based upon consistent evidence of effective practices. Team members communicate reflections, comments, and feedback through tools and rubrics provided in VAT.

The team collaborative analysis provides more extensive results than a traditional observation and feedback cycle. In this, progressing through the ERDM stages leads to a course of action driving allocation of scarce resources for professional learning. The beginning teacher may attend 'general' after school sessions helping new teachers become acclimated to school norms. More importantly, this teacher has a defined need to work with a mentor on how to use authentic problems rather than a sequence of procedures to facilitate student learning of probability concepts. The beginning teacher and mentor work through the ERDM stages together focusing first on simple then compound, independent events of probability. During the next formal observation a trail of implementation and refinement is presented using the wealth of evidence collected including video of practices demonstrating progress and changes in instructional materials.

The VAT interface provides tools for accessing, analyzing, and reflecting on the same video evidence across multiple stakeholders. Raters and practitioners identify and clarify problem evidence and contexts, establish goals, develop and elaborate evidence, and refine their understanding of key relationships by applying a lens (e.g., specific standards, benchmarks, or rubrics) to equate and reflect upon. The reflection provides an opportunity for the rater and practitioner to characterize the context in which problems are observed (or presumed) and evidence captured, document practices, associate specific standards with evidence, and share, enact and assess the impact of refinements in practice.

ISSUES AND FURTHER PROSPECTS

ERDM implementation both offers significant potential and raises important issues. In this section, we address ERDM's logistics, uses, technical requirements, and future.

Logistics: Planning and Implementation

Successful planning and implementation is influenced by the perspectives, motives, and, perhaps most importantly, preparedness of raters and practitioners. Thoughtful implementation of ERDM stages requires significant planning—potentially a significant change in practice for both raters and practitioners. Raters and participants, whether self, peer, or supervisors providing formal or informal assessments, must engage in serious planning and disciplined implementation. They need to identify target priorities, map events systematically onto the school calendar, collect and analyze diverse evidence, and act to improve both their methods and outcomes. A great deal of time and effort is invested in preparing for as well as implementing ERDM stages. The logistical issues in using direct evidence methods in typical teacher education and school curriculum structures are also significant. They require that both raters and practitioners dedicate a greater portion of their time and energy to improvement of educational practices and outcomes. Teachers as well as administrators need to allocate additional time and resources to informal self- and peer improvement of teaching practices in settings where time and resources are already overtaxed. Lacking commitment, we have little reason to expect that either teaching practices or student performance will seriously change for the better; clearly, something must give. ERDM is not "easy" to plan or implement in any sense, but we believe it represents significant potential to assess practices systematically and improve the outcomes of those practices.

Use: Informed Consent, Ownership, and Security

The use of evidence—authentic teaching learning practices keyed to specific student performance data—raises many legal and ethical issues. Should teachers, as well as students and parents, be required to participate in an approach where their moment-to-moment actions in a classroom are recorded and scrutinized in fine detail? Who "owns" video evidence of classroom practices? Can the evidence be used for other purposes, such as to document student behavior or to document teacher "unprofessional" behaviors? Does or should only ERDM-captured evidence count? Have the presumably "causal" links between teacher practice and student outcomes been verified, and have other worthy practices been inadvertently undervalued? How secure is the wealth of emerging student and teacher evidence? To some, such comprehensive systems conjure images of Big Brother, with a frightening potential for misappropriation.

As the ERDM community grows, we must engage in thoughtful conversation about how to use the methods and tools in ways that support, grow confidence, and set a path of success for teachers while protecting and ensuring each from abuse. Laws mandate, ethical standards require, and society expects strict measures to protect the identity and safeguard the rights of users, but violations involving personally identifiable data, pervasive technology and unsecured networks remain. We must address ethical and legal issues related to appropriate and reasonable use, security, and data access. We need a code of conduct—a set of assurances, clearly delineating the intended use of direct evidence to support improvements in teaching and learning if we hope to enlist the support of parents and educators alike.

Technical Requirements: Storage and Sharing

VAT implementation, especially video evidence of classroom practices, requires technical support. Considering the potential for pervasive use of VAT methods permitting all raters and practitioners, even the technological neophyte, to contribute and/or use direct video evidence of teaching practices, storage and data management requirements accelerate dramatically. The problems became apparent in the 2000 round of U.S. Department of Education PT3 program funding, when many projects developed libraries of video examples depicting exemplary technology integration classroom practices. Individual personnel addressed local issues that were, ironically, faced by virtually all projects, and generally failed to adequately consider the technological demands associated with hosting, sharing or supporting such systems. In addition, alternative approaches to providing or supporting access, such as centralized access to distributed resources, were largely unaddressed. These issues remain, though the continued acceleration of storage media, bandwidth, and computing processing power has mitigated them to some extent. We must use our collective resources to develop and test scalable models for VAT and similar systems, standardizing metadata tagging strategies (e.g., Shareable Content Object Reference Model—SCORM) and better utilizing the grid's capabilities for educational purposes and distributed storage (See http://www.gridcomputing.com).

Future: Sustainability

To be sustainable, an innovation must either clearly meet a defined need not already addressed sufficiently by an existing solution, or improve existing processes such that stakeholders recognize the need for, and adopt or adapt, the innovation. Thus far, teacher education faculty have experienced significant improvements through the increased quantity and quality of their observations. Using ERDM tools, preservice and induction teachers traditionally required to videotape their lessons, can observe and measure their progress and focus their efforts to improve. They can request that specific teaching approaches be observed and analyzed independent of day-time availability of a peer or supervisor, and can collaboratively reflect on their development with professionals whose expertise they value and trust. Yet, for each of these and other significant potentials, ERDM methods and tools require equally significant changes in traditional practices. It seems unlikely that, as an add-on or supplementary set of activities, such approaches would either be embraced or effective. Rather, to be sustainable, it needs to be integral to teacher improvement, and systematically linked to every stage of the teacher professional continuum from initial preparation efforts to induction and beyond. Sustainability is ensured by becoming systematized within, rather than marginalized from the continuous cycle of professional growth, and the need to link evidence of teacher practice with student performance.

CONCLUSIONS

The conceptual framework for continuous professional development, and stages associated with implementing ERDM for portfolio development, provide important potential for improving the practices of teacher education faculty, preparing teachers, mentors, and inservice teachers. Interestingly, the same methodology and tools offer the same potential for improving the practices of those charged with supporting or evaluating teacher practices in everyday settings. Our E-TEACH participants include teacher educators, faculty supervisors, and preservice teachers in Science Education, Elementary Education, Special Education, Educational Psychology, and Instructional Technology. Teacher educators in Science Education programs, for example, have begun to rethink the teacher preparation experience both from the perspective of rater and practitioner; similar changes are anticipated among school-level leaders who have considerable influence on the emergence of, but the fewest tools to support, the development and refinement of teacher practices. The challenges are indeed daunting, but the promise and potential just as compelling. Given the state of education, and the clamor for both greater accountability and improvement, perhaps the time for evidence-based approaches to portfolios has arrived.

ACKNOWLEDGMENT

The work presented in this paper was supported in part, through funding by the U.S. Department of Education Preparing Tomorrow's Teachers to use Technology (PT3) grant (#P342A030009)

REFERENCES

Hannafin, M. J., Hill, J., & McCarthy, J. (2002). Designing resource-based learning and performance support systems. In D. Wiley (Ed.), *The instructional use of learning objects* (pp. 99–129). Bloomington, IN: AECT.

Hill, J., Hannafin, M. J., & Recesso, P. (2007). Creating a patchwork quilt for teaching and learning: The use of learning objects in teacher education. In P. Northrup (Ed), *Learning objects for instruction: Design and evaluation* (pp. 261–279). Hershey, PA: Idea Group, Inc.

International Society for Technology in Education (ISTE). (2001). *ISTE/NCATE Standards for Candidate Proficiency Evidence.* Retrieved October 2004, from http://cnets.iste.org/ncate/pdf/tech_fac_R.pdf

National Commission on Teaching and America's Future. (1996). *What Matters Most: Teaching for America's Future.* Retrieved October 2004, from http://www.nctaf.org/documents/nctaf/WhatMattersMost.pdf

National Council for Accreditation of Teacher Education (NCATE) (2003). *Assessing Education Candidate Performance: A Look at Changing Practices.* Retrieved October 2004, from http://ncate.org/institutions/publicationsbooks.asp

National Council of Teachers of Mathematics (NCTM). (1998). *NCTM Program Standards.* Retrieved October 2004, from http://ncate.org/ProgramStandards/NCTM/nctm-98.pdf

National Science Teachers Association (NSTA). (1998). *NSTA Standards for science teacher preparation.* Retrieved October 2004, from http://www.nvc.vt.edu/nsta-ncate/november98.htm

Recker, M., Walker, A., & Lawless, K. (2003). What do you recommend? Implementation and analyses of collaborative filtering of Web resources for education. *Instructional Science, 31,* 229–316.

Recker, M., & Wiley, D. A. (2001). A non-authoritative educational metadata ontology for filtering and recommending learning objects. *Journal of Interactive Learning Environments, 1,* 1–17

Reeves, T. C., & Okey, J. R. (1996). Alternative assessment for constructivist learning environments. In B. G. Wilson (Ed.), *Constructivist learning environments: Case studies in instructional design* (pp. 191–202). Englewood Cliffs, NJ: Educational Technology Publications.

CHAPTER 3

A FIVE-STEP MODEL FOR ENHANCING ELECTRONIC TEACHING PORTFOLIOS

Andrea Bartlett
University of Hawai'i at Manoa

Dissatisfied with traditional measures of student learning, many teacher educators are implementing performance-based assessment, including portfolios, to measure teaching effectiveness. In contrast to standardized tests, performance assessment is based on a collaborative, active learning model, with the goal of assuring success on "real world" tasks (Spady & Marshall, 1991). Students are informed of performance standards, most often through rubrics, and they have opportunities to improve through self-reflection and faculty mentoring (Wigle & White, 1998).

As defined by Shulman, a teaching portfolio is: "the structured, documentary history of a set of coached or mentored acts of teaching, substantiated by samples of student portfolios, and fully realized only through reflective writing, deliberation, and conversation" (1998, p. 37). Through groundbreaking work at Stanford University's Teacher Assessment project, beginning in the 1980s, Shulman and his colleagues recommended port-

Evaluating Electronic Portfolios in Teacher Education, pages 49–62
Copyright © 2009 by Information Age Publishing

folios as a way to provide a broader, more contextualized view of teaching than is possible with standardized tests.

Although relatively new, teaching portfolios have grown in popularity with the increased demand by national, state, and local accreditation bodies for tangible artifacts of teachers' competencies. In the United States, teachers submit portfolios when applying for National Board for Professional Teaching Standards certification, and many teacher education programs prepare accreditation portfolios (McLaughlin & Vogt, 1996). Portfolios are also used to document student teaching, show in-service development, and apply for teaching positions. As a result, more and more undergraduate and graduate education majors are creating teaching portfolios (Sanders, 2000).

With new technologies available, electronic portfolios are rapidly replacing paper-based portfolios (Derham & Diperna, 2007). Constantino and De Lorenzo (2002) compared electronic and traditional portfolios.

> The electronic portfolio, just like the paper-based portfolio, is a carefully selected collection of exemplary documents that highlights a teacher's best work and accomplishments. However, unlike the paper-based portfolio, the electronic portfolio is a multimedia approach that allows the teacher to present teaching, learning and reflective artifacts in a variety of formats (audio, video, graphics, and text). (p. 48)

In contrast to bulky notebooks, electronic portfolios may be stored on CD-ROMs or the World Wide Web (Kovalchick, Milman & Elizabeth, 1998).

Electronic portfolios have many advantages over traditional portfolios. Digital and Web-based formats make them easier to update, transport and store. Electronic portfolios may also include a wide variety of artifacts that are easily cross-referenced (Yost, Brzycki & Onyett, 2002). As students use technology to create graphics and link artifacts, they are better able to see interconnections and understand their teaching development in terms of program standards (Norton-Meier, 2003). Equally important, pre-service teachers learn technology skills they can use in their classrooms, and gain confidence in their teaching abilities beyond what is accomplished with traditional portfolios (Kilbane & Milman, 2003).

CONTEXT AND PARTICIPANTS

Impressed by the literature cited above, I implemented electronic portfolios with two groups of pre-service teachers, one undergraduate (Bartlett, 2002; Bartlett & Sherry, 2004/05, 2006) and one graduate (Bartlett, 2006). To learn the technology skills needed to create electronic portfolios, I participated in technology workshops and weekly one-on-one tutoring sessions offered through a Preparing Tomorrow's Teachers to use Technology (PT3) grant in our College. A graduate technology student, also available through the grant, provided guidance and in-class support.

Since the full 5-step model was used with the pre-service graduate students, I will present that data in this chapter. This group of 22 graduate pre-service teachers held bachelors' degrees in fields other than education. Most of the students were Asian American and female. Their highly selective program led to a Masters' degree in education and certification in either elementary or secondary education.

Following a weeklong orientation and 2-week classroom immersion, students spent 2 days per week in classrooms and participated in field and integrated inquiry-based seminars (3 and 6 hours, respectively) during the first two semesters. The third semester was full-time student teaching, followed by a semester-long paid internship. As one of two Cohort Coordinators, I taught seminars and supervised field experiences during their 2-year program.

Most students began their programs with limited technology backgrounds and, thus, required support while creating their portfolios. During the 2-year program, the graduate students learned to use PowerPoint, make Web pages, conduct Internet research and create digital movies while conducting research and presenting ideas to the class. In addition to time spent learning technology, the students devoted 42 hours of class time over three semesters (16%) to creating electronic portfolios. One technology graduate student assisted me during classes and the 16 hours of open lab held in the final weeks of the project.

Portfolios included the following components: welcome page, resume, teaching philosophy, self-evaluation based on state teacher standards, instructional units, research activities, and career goals. Students used documents, digital photographs, video clips, and scanned student work samples to present their teaching development.

The original assignment was to create individual designs using the Web-based software, DreamWeaver. When this proved too difficult for some students, the technology assistant created a template for those who wanted to use it.

EVALUATING ELECTRONIC TEACHING PORTFOLIOS: A FIVE-STEP APPROACH

This section summarizes an evaluation model developed over the 2-year program. The 5 steps involved: (a) a rubric to assess individual portfolios, (b) qualitative data on students' perceptions of the assignment; (c) (dwa) qualitative data on advantages and disadvantages of electronic portfolios,

(d) quantitative data on changes in technology knowledge/attitudes, and (e) qualitative data on students' technology use as beginning teachers. The purpose of the model was to monitor the effectiveness of the electronic portfolio process and to determine whether the project was worth the time spent.

Step 1: Rubric Evaluation of Electronic Portfolios

Rubrics provide an effective way to inform students of what is expected. In my teacher education courses, I have found rubrics lead to better final projects and make grading easier. Therefore, I developed a rubric that differentiated "meets" and "exceeds" expectations for each portfolio component (see Appendix 3.1). Graduate students received the rubric early in their program and suggested changes, which I made in the final instrument. Students used the rubric to evaluate a peer and themselves and to make portfolio revisions before final submission.

Step 2: Qualitative Evaluation of Electronic Portfolio Assignment

I conducted a qualitative study to capture students' perceptions regarding the effectiveness of the assignment after they completed their portfolios. Students responded to 3 open-ended questions, asking what they learned from creating their portfolios, how the assignment could have been improved, and how they planned to use their portfolios.

Step 3: Qualitative Evaluation of Students' Perceptions of Electronic Portfolios

Students also responded to 2 open-ended questions regarding perceived advantages and disadvantages of electronic portfolios.

Step 4: Quantitative Evaluation of Technology Knowledge and Views

After completing portfolios, students rated how their technology knowledge, interest, and attitudes changed over the program's first three semesters. Students used 10-point scales to judge where they were when they entered the program and at the time of the survey.

Step 5: Qualitative Evaluation of Technology Use During Classroom Teaching

Students completed a Technology Use Survey after one semester of full-time teaching. The purpose of this instrument was to learn how teachers who created electronic portfolios used technology in their teaching.

DATA ANALYSIS

To analyze qualitative data, I parsed and categorized students' written responses. I read and reread until categories emerged, and tallied each categorized segment to provide a breakdown of students' comments regarding their degree of satisfaction (Glaser & Strauss, 1967; Strauss, 1987).

For each item on the Technology Knowledge and Views Survey, I calculated means. Then, I determined gains by comparing ratings from "when you entered the College of Education" to ratings for "now."

FINDINGS

Qualitative Evaluation of Electronic Portfolio Assignment

When asked what they learned from the electronic portfolio assignment, 15 of the 22 students reported "to use technology," and 6 stated "to use technology to organize and present ideas." Five students learned about the "disadvantages of technology." Two students said they learned each of the following: "how to apply technology to teaching," "self-evaluation," and "nothing."

Students also wrote recommendations for improving the assignment. When asked how the electronic portfolio assignment could have been more effective, 15 students responded "more or differently timed technology instruction." Nine students suggested clearer guidelines, 7 wanted more time/different timing to create portfolios, and 6 thought sample electronic portfolios/templates should be provided sooner. Less frequently mentioned were: more/different equipment (2), availability of software at home (2), more sharing of portfolios (1) and more explanation of purposes/types of portfolios (1).

When asked how they planned to use their electronic portfolios in the future, 15 students said they would use them to apply for teaching positions. In addition, 10 students wrote they would keep updating their portfolios, and 4 planned to use them for reflecting on teaching development.

Fewer students stated they would use electronic portfolios in their teaching (2) or to apply for graduate school (1). One student stated he/she did not plan to use the electronic portfolio.

Qualitative Evaluation of Students' Perceptions of Electronic Portfolios

When asked about the advantages of creating electronic portfolios, 16 students responded: "electronic portfolios are more powerful and convenient than traditional portfolios." Students also saw the portfolios as a way to showcase their technology knowledge (9), teaching ability (3), and creativity (1). They viewed electronic portfolios as being useful for job searches (6), learning about technology (3), and self-evaluation (1).

As for disadvantages, 19 students found creating electronic portfolios to be time consuming, and 9 students reported difficulties using equipment. Students also feared principals (7) and others viewing their portfolios (7) might have equipment problems. Six students saw the amount of instruction and support needed as negatives, and one student was concerned that computers are not available in public schools.

Quantitative Evaluation of Technology Knowledge and Views

Students reported improvements in all aspects of their technology knowledge (see Table 3.1). Highest levels of growth were in video editing, Web

TABLE 3.1   Means for Items on Technology Knowledge and Views Survey (N = 22)

Item	Before program	After program	Change
Knowledge: Word processing	9.05	9.18	+.13
Knowledge: PowerPoint	7.09	8.18	+1.09
Knowledge: Web software	3.05	6.95	+3.90
Knowledge: Video editing	3.18	7.59	+4.41
Knowledge: Using images	5.68	7.68	+2.00
Knowledge: Technology	5.91	7.84	+1.93
Interest: Technology	6.77	8.00	+1.23
Attitude: Technology in education	6.91	8.14	+1.23
Application: Planned application to teaching	7.00	8.05	+1.05

Note: Scale: 1 (low) to 10 (high)

software, and image use. Interest in learning technology, attitude toward using technology in education, and degree to which students planned to use technology in their future teaching also improved.

Qualitative Evaluation of Technology Use during Classroom Teaching

Fifteen of the 22 pre-service teachers responded to this survey at the end of their 4th semester internship. Interns had sole responsibility for their teaching assignments but were supervised at least weekly by university faculty. Responses to this survey are presented by question below.

Do you think technology experiences during teacher education helped you use the technology you needed as a teacher? If yes, which experiences helped you? If no, what would have been more helpful? Seven interns stated that technology experiences during their teacher education program helped them use technology once they became teachers; 5 said "no," and 3 said "yes/no" or "neutral." Of those responding "yes," helpful experiences included iMovie (4), the electronic portfolio (3), PowerPoint (2), Web pages (1), videotaped lessons (1), and Mac use (1).

Interns who answered "no" suggested the following experiences would have helped them implement technology: PowerPoint, grade sheets, WebQuests, Excel, word processing, children's software, Photoshop, strategies to manage students using technology, and ways to use technology in classrooms.

One "yes/no" responder wrote: "We had some experience with technology, but I think we could have done more." The second "yes/no" response was, "Yes, I learned more than I previously knew about the programs we used. The experience also made me more interested in integrating technology," and "No, I didn't have a strong foundation in technology to begin with and felt that the programs we used were above my level of understanding. I also feel we did not have sufficient time to practice what we learned, so I know I would not be able to do something like the e-portfolio by myself." The intern who wrote "neutral" went on to say, "I don't think it impacted my teaching at all."

Do you think creating an electronic portfolio helped you use the technology you needed as a teacher? If yes, why do you think so and how did it help you? If no, what could have been changed to make it more helpful? Eight interns answered "no," the electronic portfolio assignment did not help them use technology, 5 said "yes," and 2 were "unsure" or "neutral." Two of the interns responding "no" wrote they did not believe they could make an electronic portfolio on their own. One student said there were too many changes in the electronic portfolio assignment, and another said she was not certain she would use the same technology in teaching that we used for the portfolios. Yet another intern recommended use of more user friendly, or children's, software.

Two students who responded "yes" stated they found DreamWeaver helpful. The following experiences were found helpful by one student each: movie making, Web page creation, and ways to engage students visually. These benefits of electronic portfolios were given by interns: way to present self as a teacher (1), can be posted for job hunting (1), and improved my reflection process (1).

The intern who wrote in "neutral" stated: "It made me create a portfolio, but I still think a paper-based one would be fine, too."

What changes in your previous field experiences would have helped you use technology more and more effectively? Interns had 5 different recommendations for changes in their field experiences that would encourage technology use: requirements to teach a technology lesson in a class (3) and develop curriculum that included technology (1), observations of classrooms in which technology is used (1), more computers in classrooms (1), and field experiences in technologically advanced schools (1).

Some recommendations related to the technology assignments and what was needed to complete them. Interns thought there should be technology classes or workshops (2); more time to practice (2); more help in workshops (1); simpler (1), classroom-based assignments (2) with each step typed out (1); and College provided software (1). Interns also stated smaller projects should lead up to a major project (1), and there should be access to technology every day (1).

What are your short and long term goals regarding technology use? In their teaching, interns planned to have students create electronic portfolios (3); post class materials (2) and student assignments (1); use cameras in teaching (2); use filmmaking as a communication tool for students (2); teach children to use PowerPoint (1), word processing (1), and the Internet for research (1); create templates for students (1); continue collaborating with students on technology assignments (1); and use more technology with students (2).

Interns also planned to use the electronic portfolio for job interviews (1), use online journals for research (1), retrieve lesson plans online (1), make Web pages (1), write grants to improve technology access (1), use technology daily (1) and be a technology coordinator (1). Other professional uses of technology included: continue fine tuning Internet research (1) and continue using e-mail (1).

Some interns' responses reveal a continuing interest in learning about technology, specifically software (2), hardware (1), and Internet use with young children (1). Other interns stated they hope to receive more training (2), become more comfortable with technology (1), keep up with current technology (1), and use more technology in my personal life (1).

CONCLUSIONS

The 5-step model provides a useful framework for assessing electronic port-folios. On the positive side, students saw advantages of creating electronic portfolios, and they believed their knowledge and attitudes toward class-rooms applications increased during the process. The model also shows students applied technology in a number of ways in their first four months of teaching, and they hoped to increase technology use in the future.

More important for program improvement, the model identified poten-tial areas for change. Based on difficulties students faced, I will recommend assignment changes in these areas: set explicit goals for portfolios, clarify guidelines, and provide adequate time and support. Then, I will recom-mend ways to enhance the 5-step model itself.

Recommended Improvements in the Electronic Portfolio Assignment

Explicit Goals. Students were most likely to state they learned to use tech-nology—one important goal of the project. However, it was disappointing so few students mentioned other major goals of the assignment, such as learning to self-evaluate and apply technology to teaching.

This finding indicates the technology aspects of the assignment over-whelmed other considerations. In line with students' sensible recommen-dations, I will select easier software, possibly in collaboration with students; provide a template when introducing the portfolio; and guide students' reflections for greater concentration on elements of effective teaching. As Willis (2001) cautioned: "Technology should be in the background; it can never be *The Focus*" (p. 4).

Similarly, students in this study believed they were most likely to use their portfolios for job searches. Although this is an anticipated use for aspiring teachers, applications to teaching and reflecting on teaching development were less likely to be mentioned. This finding supports the previous conclu-sion that classroom applications and self-evaluation techniques need to be emphasized during the portfolio process.

Clear Guidelines. Students' responses to the qualitative survey show I could have been even clearer about expectations for the electronic portfolio as-signment. Other researchers (Lamson, Thomas, Aldrich & King, 2001) found pre-service teachers need to be informed "early and often" about electronic portfolio requirements and expectations. Even when pre-service teachers were given templates, these same researchers concluded:

Change in the content, the focus, or the format of the electronic portfolio is likely to be necessary as goals are changed or more efficient methods for construction are discovered. The evolving process can be frustrating to candidates and faculty involved. When undertaking the implementation of electronic portfolios, continue to focus on the benefits of utilizing the multimedia format for professional portfolios with the understanding that flexibility throughout the learning process greatly enhances the final outcome. (p. 7)

With this in mind, I plan to provide as much information and guidance as possible, while leaving room for change as the project develops. One way to clarify expectations is to develop rubrics with students, instead of just seeking their recommendations on my draft. By participating in rubric development, students will gain a better understanding of what can be achieved through various electronic portfolio components. To further clarify expectations, I plan to use the rubric for peer and self-evaluation throughout the process and not just near the end. Although it is difficult to find time for such lengthy analyses and communications, creating a true "portfolio culture" demands it (Duschl & Gitomer, 1991, p. 840).

Time and Support. Students called for more time to work on portfolios, spaced evenly throughout the program. Although students completed segments as they progressed, they scrambled in their last month of student teaching—an already stressful time—to put the final portfolio together. Students' comments show I need to make a greater time commitment to creating portfolios than the 42 hours (16%) of class time allotted with this cohort and frontload that time as much as possible.

Upon reviewing this data, I also reconsidered how class time was used. Although the rest of the program was inquiry-based, I presented technology via the traditional model of teacher presentation, student practice and student application. Instead, I plan to have students use their reasoning skills by giving more time for exploration and self-determination (Simpson & Payne, 1999). This change would minimize reliance on technology and content assistance, and make students more responsible for their own learning.

Adjustments to the 5-Step Assessment Model

Although the assessment model provided a broader view of electronic portfolios in teacher education than is currently available, this study shows how the model could be further improved. As stated earlier, pre-service teachers should participate in rubric development to increase their understanding and ownership of the portfolio process.

The study underscores the importance of assessing pre-service teachers' technology skills and monitoring their perceptions throughout the electronic portfolio process. Instead of having the pre-service teachers assess their growth in technology skills after creating portfolios, it would have been far better to administer this instrument as a pre-test; then, periodically throughout the process, thus enabling faculty to adjust the technology requirements and levels of support, based on pre-service teachers' growing confidence and capabilities. Similarly, changes based on more frequent assessments (e.g., twice a semester) of the pre-service teachers' perceptions of the electronic portfolio assignment are likely to result in a more meaningful portfolio process.

While it is essential to know students' perceptions of assignments during and after completion, it is equally important to discern if they are able to apply what they learned in teaching contexts. In spite of the well-known challenges of first-year teaching, some of the graduate students applied technology as interns and held ambitious goals for future use. In fact, two interns actually had children in their classes create electronic portfolios. It would be interesting to reassess this group of teachers after five years of teaching—once they have more of a handle on classroom management and other issues—to see how their technology use develops.

As hoped, application of the 5-step evaluation model illuminates changes that further enhance the electronic portfolio process and the model itself. The many colleges rushing to implement electronic portfolios for student and program assessment would be well advised to evaluate the portfolio creation process and make similar adjustments as needed. Without adequate evaluation, it is unlikely that electronic portfolios, or other technology implementation, will be successful. Without thorough evaluations, such projects may even backfire, leaving students with negative attitudes toward technology and their teacher education programs.

Taken together, the qualitative and quantitative evaluation measures presented here will help teacher educators implement electronic portfolios, and possibly other technology innovations, in a way that is most beneficial for our students. As Willis (2001) pointed out, "The goal of technology integration . . . is a moving and ill-defined target" (p. 11). Our faculty did, indeed, "end with a vision" of what should follow (Willis, 2001, p. 10). As hard as we worked on what we have accomplished so far, there is still much more to do, given our nation's need for technologically proficient teachers. Electronic portfolios address this need by engaging pre-service teachers in a dynamic use of instructional technology.

REFERENCES

Bartlett, A. (2002). Preparing preservice teachers to implement performance assessment and technology through electronic portfolios. *Action in Teacher Education, 24*(1), 90–97.

Bartlett, A. (2006). It was hard work, but it was worth it: A case study of e-portfolios in teacher education. In A. Jafari & C. W. Kaufman (Eds.), *Handbook of research on e-portfolios,* (pp. 325–337). New York: Idea Group.

Bartlett, A., & Sherry, A.C. (2004/05). Non-technology-savvy pre-service teachers' perceptions of electronic teaching portfolios. *Contemporary Issues in Technology and Teacher Education, [Online serial] 4(2).* Retrieved July 16, 2007, from http://www.citejournal.org/vol4/iss2/currentpractice/article1.cfm

Constantino, P. M., & De Lorenzo, M. N. (2002). *Developing a professional teaching portfolio.* Boston: Allyn & Bacon.

Derham, C., & Diperna, J. (2007). Digital professional portfolios of preservice teaching: An initial study of score reliability and validity. *Journal of Technology and Teacher Education, 15*(3), 363–381.

Duschl, R. A., & Gitomer, D. H. (1991). Epistemological perspectives on conceptual change: Implications for educational practice. *Journal of Research in Science Teaching, 28*(9), 839–858.

Glaser, B. G., & Strauss, A. L. (1967). *The discovery of grounded theory: Strategies for qualitative research.* Chicago, IL: Aldine.

Kilbane, C. R., & Milman, N. B. (2003). *The digital teaching portfolio handbook: A how-to guide for educators.* Boston: Allyn & Bacon.

Kovalchick, A., Milman, N. B., & Elizabeth, M. (1998). *Instructional strategies for integrating technology: Electronic journals and technology portfolios as facilitators for self-efficacy and reflection in preservice teachers.* (ERIC Reproduction Service: ED421115).

Lamson, S., Thomas, K. R., Aldrich, J., & King, A. (2001). *Assessing preservice candidates' web-based electronic portfolios.* (ERIC Document Reproduction Service No. ED458202).

McLaughlin, M., & Vogt, M. E. (1996). *Portfolios in teacher education.* Newark, DE: International Reading Association.

Norton-Meier, L. A. (2003). To efoliate or not to efoliate? The rise of the electronic portfolio in teacher education. *Journal of Adolescent & Adult Literacy, 46*(6), 516–518.

Sanders, M. E. (2000). Web-based portfolios for technology education: A personal case study. *Journal of Technology Studies, 26*(1), 11–18.

Shulman, L. (1998). Teacher portfolios: A theoretical activity. In N. Lyons. (Ed.), *With portfolio in hand: Validating the new teacher professionalism,* (pp. 23–38). New York: Teachers College.

Simpson, M., & Payne, F. (1999). Using information and communications technology as a pedagogical tool: Who educates the educators? *Journal of Teacher Education, 25*(3), 247–258.

Spady, W., & Marshall, K. (1991). Beyond traditional outcomes-based education. *Educational Leadership, 49,* 67–72.

Strauss, A. L. (1987). *Qualitative analysis for social scientists.* Cambridge, England: University Press.

Wigle, S. E., & White, G. T. (1998). Conceptual frameworks, portfolio assessment and faculty mentoring: Bridges to standards-based teacher education programs. *Action in Teacher Education, 20*(3), 39–49.

Willis, J. (2001). Foundational assumptions for information technology and teacher education. *Contemporary Issues in Technology and Teacher Education [Online serial] 1(3)*. Retrieved July 16, 2007, from http://www.citejournal.org/vol1/iss3/editorials/article1.htm

Yost, N., Brzycki, D., & Onyett, L. C. (2002). *Electronic portfolios on a grand scale.* Paper presented at Society for Information Technology and Teacher Education (SITE) 2002. Retrieved July 16, 2007, from http://www.editlib.org/index.cfm?fuseaction=Reader.ViewAbstract&paper_id=10855

APPENDIX 3.1   Electronic Portfolio Rubric

Portfolio of: _____   Reviewed by: _____   Date: _____

Section	Meets expectations	Pts	Exceeds expectations	Pts	Score
Welcome page	Attractive introduction to your portfolio. Identifying information and purpose clearly stated.	3	Eye-catching and original. Shows what is special about you. Effective use of images and/or movies.	4	
Résumé	Education and work experience presented clearly.	3	N/A	3	
Teaching philosophy	Describes your ideas about how children learn and how you plan to teach. Clear format and grammatically correct.	9	Explains theories and philosophers related to your ideas and why you agree	10	
Unit	Complete unit with Content/Performance Standards and Teacher Standards, assessment, and procedures. Evaluations of children and self for each lesson and unit overall. Samples of children's work.	9	Particularly detailed procedures and in-depth reflections. Effective use of images and/or movies.	10	
Self-evaluation	All 10 Teacher Standards with supporting examples from you teaching	9	Effective use of images and/or movies.	10	
Research	All sections of your research proposal	10	N/A	10	
Career goals	Attractive closing page that summarizes your portfolio	2	Eye-catching and original. Effective use of images and/or movies.	3	

Strengths and suggestions for improvement:

CHAPTER 4

TOO NEW A TALE TO TELL?

Issues in Evaluating E-Portfolio Systems and Implementations

Bruce Havelock
RMC Research Corporation

CONTEXT: LESSONS IN E-PORTFOLIO EVALUATION

RMC Research Corporation serves as external evaluator for a wide range of education clients, including the U.S. Department of Education (USDOE) and several State and Local Educational Agencies (SEAs and LEAs). After RMC completed a national evaluation of the Preparing Tomorrow's Teachers to Use Technology (PT3) grant program in 2002, I managed and staffed external evaluation research programs for several PT3 grantees over the following years 2002–2005, involving dozens of teacher preparation institutions. The three PT3 grant projects selected for discussion in this chapter all used e-portfolios as a core component of their strategies for supporting teacher fluency with technology. As the work of evaluation was in no way a solitary effort, throughout this chapter I use "we" to refer to the the teams at RMC Research Corporation who work to better understand many innovative applications of technology in education settings, e-portfolios among them.

Evaluating Electronic Portfolios in Teacher Education, pages 63–90
Copyright © 2009 by Information Age Publishing
All rights of reproduction in any form reserved.

Part of the work of evaluation involved collecting and analyzing data that gave insight into the real impact of these portfolios. As researchers, we wanted to understand how pre-service teachers and their instructors became comfortable and adept at using technology to support high-quality teaching and learning. Using portfolio assessment, educators were deconstructing education itself, breaking experiences down to time segment captures of their work in practice. Learners at all levels of the system struggled to balance environmental pressures (Zhao & Frank, 2003), their varying technology experiences and attitudes, and the challenge of structuring and comprehending complex portraits of emerging expertise in teaching.

While trying to understand and document the impact of e-portfolios in these teacher education settings, the often limited uses of e-portfolios naturally constrained the body of meaningful evidence available. Simple quantitative measures of use, fluency, and perceived value revealed little about the portfolios themselves. Many e-portfolios we reviewed consisted of either an empty shell or a perfunctory and superficial set of artifacts showing no evidence of thoughtful assembly. Basic measures of quality generally revealed that nonexistent or poor portfolios far outnumbered the exemplars in most settings. However, in some settings we observed truly transformative and sustained uses of e-portfolios as critically reflective tools for ongoing growth, and the potential for value demonstrated by these best practices was inspiriting. We were energized by the transformative potential of e-portfolios as richly detailed assessment systems, yet studying these implementations often proved frustrating. Teacher candidates and their instructors struggled, both with new technologies and with the challenges of explicitly linking their educational knowledge, beliefs, and practices through a set of created artifacts.

In representing programs through evaluation research, we aimed to disprove a null hypothesis that a given e-portfolio system did not support teacher candidate growth in meaningful ways. However, that hypothesis was difficult to disprove. While each of the e-portfolio implementations we studied had what might be called its "crusader advocates," or individuals who served as champions for a transformative vision of assessment and growth in teaching, many of the implementations revealed inconsistent use, frustrated students, sporadic support for implementation, and no clear results for either good or ill.

Factors external to teacher learning often influenced e-portfolio implementations, including accreditation processes, administrative pressures to use technology, or various budgetary enablers and constraints. Much of the systemic conflict, negotiation, and compromise that accompanied the e-portfolio implementation and piloting processes where we observed them centered on the use of the supporting technologies themselves. Discussions of enacted pedagogy and instructional quality often were mediated by issues of Internet access and general technological fluency.

When seeking to understand the wider systemic impacts of e-portfolios on teacher preparation programs, the evidence reflected the often uncertain focus, vague goals, and nonspecific strategies that drove e-portfolio implementation in the settings we observed. In these cases, a close look at the real implications of technology for portfolio assessments rode backseat to more pressing institutional needs related to institutional politics, resulting in conflicting messages from administrative leadership and instructors about why e-portfolios were being integrated into preservice teacher requirements.

Though confusion plagued many e-portfolio implementation settings we studied, other such implementations blossomed. In convoluted settings, small self-selected cadres of teachers were embracing the unprecedented power of e-portfolios for documenting how they taught, the impacts that their instruction was having on students, and what students could learn. They used e-portfolios to capture as faithfully as they could the essential tensions and questions that drove their instruction, and to challenge their own thinking and assumptions about what constitutes best practices in teaching specific content to specific audiences. Model e-portfolios were certainly developed by engaged and motivated teacher candidates, but the short duration of typical e-portfolio engagements (averaging 6–10 months) constrained the evidence available to document long-term outcomes and learning experiences. While focusing on model or showcase e-portfolios illustrated the potential of given e-portfolio toolsets, it did not represent the experiences of most teacher candidates and teacher educators in the settings we studied.

In this chapter, I provide brief overviews of e-portfolio implementations in three distinct teacher education settings where RMC Research was contracted to evaluate the overall preservice teacher technology integration project. By examining the contextual pressures, adoption trajectories, and limited results evident across these settings, my hope is to provide a foundation for future discussions about how researchers and practitioners can document and understand the real ways that technology systems intersect with institutional and educational goals. The centrality of e-portfolios to project aims in each of the settings we studied varied from minimal to fundamental, but in each case, we were, as evaluators, charged with understanding and presenting the processes and impacts of change in a particular setting. The settings themselves that became units of analysis in our research ranged from clusters of institutions, to cadres of university faculty, to individual K–12 classrooms. I hope that the lessons learned in these settings can provide insight for researchers and practitioners in equally varied settings.

The primary purpose of this chapter is to illustrate through example how general evaluation practices and principles can support effective practice in the implementation of electronic portfolio projects. Many of the issues raised in this chapter are not unique to e-portfolios. However, by applying sound evaluation practice to their implementations, practitioners in e-portfolio settings will be able to insure that their impact is documented, their successes are repeatable, and their challenges and lessons learned are systematically incorporated for continuous improvement.

EVALUATION ACROSS A RANGE OF E-PORTFOLIO CONTEXTS

The three implementations chosen for discussion here produced a range of work products or artifacts. Artifacts produced by targeted participants included a variety of simple and complex uses of various technologies that in 2004 had been either adopted to support or created specifically for e-portfolio assembly and presentation. Targeted audiences used PowerPoint; digital video and its enabling technologies; and online assessment technology database systems. One project of national scope developed the Personal Learning Planner (PLP)[1], a robust, complex, customizable electronic database linking standards, reflection, mentoring, and multiple iterations of work samples in an online environment. While most portfolios were created for individuals, some were for teams and organizations.

PROJECT PRESENTATION METHODOLOGY

Three projects are discussed in greater detail below. Each description includes:

- Project goals and context, including the role of e-portfolios within the project, and
- Results, implications, and lessons learned about e-portfolio implementation and evaluation best practices.

The case of the PLP contains an additional section on issues specific to PLP as a relational database designed for authentic assessment. In the first two examples, pseudonyms have been used to identify the projects. The purpose here is not to present specific research findings from the discussed setting, but to provide context for reflection on impact across contexts. Specific evaluation data and results are available in source reports and other publications (Havelock & Sherry 2003; Havelock, Gibson, & Sherry, 2003; Sherry 2004; Sherry, Havelock, & Gibson 2004; Sherry 2005).

Project SABRE: Goals and Context

Project SABRE implemented campus-wide faculty training sessions in technology at the college of education in a publicly funded state university. In addition, student mentor teams facilitated a range of technology integration practices among university faculty on individual bases. In later years, the numerous urban school districts named as project partners became more involved with the grant as members of the teaching faculty grew more comfortable in their practices with technology and carried their new interest to school districts in various ways.

Although SABRE presented and supported a range of hardware and software uses across the university campus, e-portfolios were neither required nor emphasized, and were only adopted on an experimental level by individual instructors who were interested in independent exploration of e-portfolios with their own student groups. Though it was not the norm, a few of the teacher educators in the project found that technology in their professional lives became a catalyst, authentically revitalizing and transforming their senses of career engagement and mission. As many readers will know, e-portfolios are more naturally suited than many other forms of technology use to this type of growth. A few professors in the college of education adopted the development of e-portfolio collections as course requirements.

Project SABRE: Implementation

In those classes where it was a requirement, teacher candidates in early years developed PowerPoint presentations highlighting their work in a variety of topics. The slide shows assembled by these aspiring teachers varied in both content and format; one might be a complex self-running presentation using animations, transitions, sounds, and clip art to present a worksheet developed for classroom use, another might demonstrate the features of a district-wide assessment and remediation system.

Later years saw growth in the complexity of portfolio expectations as professors wrestled with the challenge of pushing their students toward deeper professional reflection. State accreditation pressures provided the primary driver for instructors to align their work with state definitions of teacher mastery, and professors who chose to experiment with e-portfolios clearly shaped their course requirements to reflect those definitions of mastery. The externally defined teacher competency of aligning teacher practice with community needs was identified by practitioners as a clear priority for the schools districts being served, though these varied greatly in the resources available and the needs requiring teacher attention.

In this context, e-portfolio criteria were adapted to reward presentations illustrating how teacher candidates understood the school, students, teachers, and community in the schools where they worked as student teachers. Resulting student e-portfolios illustrated dress and conduct at schools, presenting dissections of lunchtime norms and rituals alongside test scores, dropout figures, and demographic data. Churches attended by the school's teachers and community families "shared the screen" with other resource agencies and contacts and the ways they supported students.

E-portfolios in project SABRE emerged naturally from teacher practice and served as one way to meet state teacher accreditation pressures. The guidelines that required teachers to embed longer-term narrative time sequences into their e-portfolios started to define, illuminate, and support their incipient growth naturally as engaged teaching professionals. These community-based presentations illustrated a point-in-time (one course semester) snapshot of student growth along a small set of valued outcomes, but the number of teacher candidates who continued independently developing their e-portfolios, or how they applied any of their portfolio-based learning to their continuing professional lives, is unknown. Though this set of e-portfolios provided a substantial record of competence along defined teacher competencies (including technology use itself), their impact at the time was limited to single course experiences. The teacher education practitioners involved here clearly aimed to support reflection through a collection of artifacts of practice. Though PowerPoint slideshows do not meet a robust definition of an e-portfolio, the groups involved did consider themselves to have successfully experimented with portfolio-based evidence of teaching results.

Project BETTER: Goals and Context

A second state-funded university more deliberately implemented e-portfolios as a defined strategy requiring teams of master teachers, teacher educators, and teacher candidates to develop bodies of evidence to document their activities and progress in meeting the university's teacher education requirements. BETTER used an off-the shelf e-portfolio system, and each team was required to use it. Leadership and technology fluency naturally varied among teams and their members, but the deliberate nature of guidelines provided by the grant assured that codified indicators of competence guided the development of artifacts from field placement. Further, the process of reflection so critical to effective learning through portfolios (cf. Barrett, 2005) became explicitly embedded into portfolio requirements. In this case, participating faculty and leadership coded the resulting portfolio products using rubrics to support qualitative coding, with each indicator demonstrating "little or no evidence," "some evidence," and "ample evidence" of mastery.

Project BETTER: Implementation

One primary project outcome was the emergence of digital video recording as a prevalent feature exercised with increasing skill over the course of the project. In these richly detailed records of practice, participants described finding abundant evidence of the impact of their work. After roughly two years of reflection, teams started articulating the links they saw between the content of the teaching methods curriculum and the techniques employed by student teachers. E-portfolios containing lesson plans, multiple video segments, and resulting student work samples became the enabling platform for abundantly rich team discussions of teaching and learning. Over time, as teachers and teacher educators gained practice with the process, their criteria for what constituted e-portfolio quality grew in complexity and depth

However, the vague rating system did not provide enough data to generalize beyond any single portfolio. As artifacts of team-based interaction, these e-portfolios were again constrained by a fixed-time endpoint. Participants all but unanimously viewed the use of video as immensely valuable for teaching and learning; in this setting, digital capture and manipulation of this basic unit of teaching practice (the classroom-based lesson segment) stimulated participants' deep reflection on quality teaching. Again, the longer-term impact of the approach to professional growth thus fostered was beyond the scope of the grant or its evaluation. BETTER made substantial progress in developing a link between teaching practice and K–12 student outcomes, combining video and e-portfolios to document and reflect on a teaching lesson similar to a lesson study model (cf. Hiebert, Gallimore, & Stigler, 2002). When teams dissolved at the grant's conclusion, there was little beyond the enthusiasm of individuals, a handful of rubric scores, and the e-portfolios themselves to indicate impact.

PLP: Goals and Context

The third described grant evaluation is the Personal Learning Planner (PLP), a highly customizable e-portfolio system developed through the Teacher Education Network (TEN), a PT3 Catalyst grant. As one of the grant's fundamental goals, TEN aimed to create a Web-based toolset that enabled sustained, high-quality feedback to improve preservice work. The PLP software itself was developed using Domino, a data structure created by IBM. It combined tools for collaboration and data gathering with tools for e-portfolio assembly and presentation. Conceptualized as a learner-centered toolset, the PLP emphasized online dialogue between learners and the people advising them. The PLP includes tools for online survey building and administration, the development of local standards and rubrics, the organization of goals and work products in relation to these standards and rubrics, the formation of learners and advisors in various online community configurations, and the creation of a completed web-based portfolio product. Developers paid explicit attention to embedding features in the PLP that allowed implementing institutions to customize the standards to which portfolio artifacts were aligned, support collaborative dialogue around learning experiences and artifacts demonstrating mastery of intended standards for knowledge and performance, and document both works in progress and finished products.

On the surface, the divergent uses of the PLP seem to contrast with e-portfolios using less flexible tools. Compared to simple presentation software, the PLP enabled a much wider range of activities related to creating and reflecting on work products. However, as in settings where other tools were used, the strongest influences on quality came more from the practitioners and their practices in context than from particular features of the toolset.

PLP: Implementation

As a system, the PLP was robust and flexible enough to support a wide range of implementation goals. In the dozens of test or pilot settings and uses, these goals took vastly different shapes. In each setting, intensive and sustained technical support was required for users to customize and maintain their dedicated PLP server; unfortunately, the minimal early scale of most test implementations rendered an effective barrier to sustained use. Basic costs associated with implementation and maintenance and uncertain projections of purpose and value left many would-be PLP users unable to persuade stakeholders in their respective settings of the PLP's potential value. Though initial interest was high, as in one setting where over 140 people arrived at a training event designed to support 30, the support needed to sustain PLP use was difficult to obtain.

One result of the many potential and actual implementation barriers was that only a few pilot implementations truly flourished or yielded long-term commitments to e-portfolios as an integrated institutional learning strategy. The institutions themselves where the PLP was used in the period 2000–2003 ranged from K–12 schools to teacher preparation institutions to other graduate and professional programs of different stripes. Yet in each test setting, only a small number of users developed portfolio content beyond a single perfunctory document posting or even an empty shell. The technological challenges of mastering this complex toolset contribute to the net effect of dozens of created portfolio "spaces" and user learning communities, but few actual collections of student work occupying that space. Though advocates and leaders created a few exemplary products, many early PLP implementations were all but empty shells.

Best practice exemplars collected from the PLP clearly identified users who had invested enough time and effort into learning and using the system to develop portfolios that authentically and powerfully catalyzed and displayed their growth and development. Such a level of use was, as in other settings, rare. Yet where it occurred, such use illustrated the potential and power of e-portfolio systems that explicitly link their assumptions and value principles to their specific structures for developing and displaying portfolio contents.

The case of the PLP highlighted the balance between the potentials of e-portfolios and the often overwhelming challenges of their use. The features of the PLP effectively required its users in 2004 to integrate high levels of fluency with technology; commitment to collaborative discourse around improvement of their work; and explicit articulation of the relationships between standards, mastery, and evidence that comprise high-quality assessment.

PLP: Additional Issues

The extensive features of the PLP as an enabling technology for e-portfolio implementation merit a deeper look. Through their work, PLP advocates and users across settings evinced in detail a collision between what we might call "e-portfolio ideals" and existing embedded cultural assumptions about technology, collaboration, accountability, and assessment. Explicit considerations and value principles embedded in the PLP provided its users with a more complex and detailed environment for structuring the process of goal setting and documentation of growth. The corresponding technological fluency required for users to fully engage the PLP's capacities proved an intimidating obstacle for many.

To illustrate, imagine that you, the reader, in whatever your work setting, were approached and informed that your workplace was adopting a new performance evaluation methodology. From here forward, you will be required to use a completely unfamiliar computer program to do each of the following:

- Complete a series of assessment quizzes and surveys periodically administered by your supervisors on different topics.
- Articulate your own goals for learning and development, then evaluate and reflect upon your attainment of those goals.
- Upload documents as evidence of both formative and summative professional learning
- Tie all of your work to a set of professional standards that you have heard about, and even own, but rarely referenced or thought about deeply.
- Share accountability for attainment of those standards by communicating with a group of your colleagues and advisors, obtaining and providing timely feedback completed and in-progress work
- Maintain evidence of your learning trajectory across multiple years.

Many present readers will certainly find this hypothetical environment deeply stimulating. However, even the most optimistic among us must acknowledge that some of our peers and colleagues might find this requirement, layered upon existing duties, a touch overwhelming. Members of the PLP's intended audience naturally enough manifested both reactions.

Further, accountability pressures in many settings actually supported these ideals. As one persistent advocate explained, "Educators in [my state] right now seem to love the idea of a matrix and portfolio where they generate the portfolio around a given set of standards or goals. With one click, I can make a matrix (of standards and goal attainment) and see at a glance exactly the areas where I need growth. That makes me a self-directed learner." By modeling her own PLP portfolio for various audiences, this advocate-user over time nurtured the adoption of an e-portfolio strategy to support learning teams (similar to Project BETTER) and institutions, inspiring leaders in a school district to adopt a portfolio model for illustrating several years of institutional growth in a "district PLP." Other PLP advocate-users shared their interest across traditional institutional lines, supporting nascent e-portfolio implementations across different university departments or school districts and service agencies.

The experiences of these advocate-users proved useful in elaborating the critical dimensions of relevance that made the PLP so potentially successful across settings. On the practical side, more successful advocates and leaders in different implementation settings emphasized a manageable subset of the potential objectives the PLP can support, using aspects of the toolset to greater and lesser degrees. Additionally, they identified key features that exhibited durable value to them in supporting their own process. For example, one advocate-user described the critical importance of reflection:

> Meaningful reflection is the key to the whole process. Without reflection, a portfolio is pretty meaningless; it's just a collection of data points. It needs to be more than just showing a collection of work to your supervisor; it should support your personal growth. . . . Seeing reflection in the context of a data point related to a goal or standard is critical. The PLP accommodates reflection extremely well. (Havelock & Sherry, 2003)

Where leaders' ideas about assessment, collaboration, and learning matched the various affordances of the PLP, implementation activity was much more likely to flourish. In all settings, the cultural or institutional practices and prior experiences of different pilot groups strongly influenced their initial engagements with the PLP. Beyond their experience with paper portfolios, different groups had varying types of norms in place surrounding many aspects of their work with the PLP. This included at various times participant conceptions of mentorship, reflection, the purpose of a portfolio-like collection of work, the relevance of such a portfolio to their jobs and careers, the idea of assessment as entailing a fixed-point evaluation of a finished product, and familiarity with and ideas about content standards. As users became more familiar with the PLP, some tentative reconsideration of norms of teaching and learning—visible through more reflective comments, active engagement with PLP work, and descriptions of such changes by program administrators—were evident as risk-taking and experimentation with the PLP was supported and encouraged.

In the absence of definite and/or comprehensible requirements, many potential participants did nothing; even where e-portfolios were required as part of teacher preparation coursework, often we found that only a few teacher candidates went beyond the minimal imposed requirements to engage in authentic and engaged use of portfolio collections to demonstrate their own growth and understanding through the practice of setting goals and reflecting on their attainment.

We hoped as evaluators that the information we provided would help administrators think critically about how to support audiences best in the complex task of integrating assessment, technology, and learning. Yet the expertise and drive required to exert fully effective leadership for that integration was often absent from implementation settings. Implementation in many settings, including some of those mentioned here, was not always framed in comprehensive or clearly articulated terms. Coherent data collection to support assertions about program efficacy was often challenging given the nebulous priorities, strategies, and intended impacts in some settings. Further, these conceptual frameworks were universally subject to change. Rather than lament these constant metamorphoses, we learned to integrate evidence about the shifting terrain of goals and impacts into the body of evidence documenting change along originally planned and predicted dimensions. We hope that the principles and observations presented here will assist researchers and practitioners working to understand and support particular e-portfolio system implementations.

EVALUATION PROCESSES AND METHODS

The three examples suggest a range of potential goals, strategies, and outcomes related to e-portfolio implementation. Evaluation provides indispensable support for any project's success and continuation by providing clear documentation of project intentions; the activities and methods used to act on those intentions; and the results in both intended and unintended areas of impact. As those three stages arguably comprise the "essential food groups" for the concerned evaluator, their implications for design and execution of evaluation studies are of primary importance here.

Program logic models (McLaughlin & Jordan, 1999) provide a simple and effective tool for conceptualizing and communicating these relationships. We have found consistently that explicitly articulated program logic serves as a foundational platform from which administrators and researchers can analyze impact and support continuous program improvement, a funding supported in evaluation literature (cf. Cooksy, Gill, & Kelly, 2001; Chen, 2004). A robust plan for formative data collection, analysis, and reporting around each stage of program implementation best assures that formative and summative evaluations catalyze and enable project success and continuation.

Any effective evaluation requires access to external perspectives and expertise (Weiss, Coffman, & Bohan-Baker, 2002). As an independent firm, RMC Research brought both of these to bear, working to build partnerships with clients that developed evaluation research as a critical pillar supporting their long-term success. In developing research strategies to accommodate the diversity and complexity of e-portfolios on different systemic levels, lessons emerged that I hope may serve educators working to develop and sustain e-portfolio implementations in any setting. These specific recommendations follow.

Cross-Evaluation Lessons: Evaluating E-portfolio Goals

Effective evaluation starts with conversation. External facilitation of early conversations can support logic model articulation or refinement, providing a common foundation for both the project activities and the evaluation strategy. Clear discussions and visual representations of program logic and the nature of the evidence that will be generated to document attainment of program goals will support a maximally effective implementation and a correspondingly strong evaluation.

As program leaders and impacted members of the audience articulate goals and guidelines for portfolio development, questions to be considered should include, at a minimum, the following:

- What goals does the institution have for e-portfolio use?
- What goals are portfolio owners expected to have?
- What assertions should the portfolio support, and how should it support them?
- What learning processes is the portfolio intended to capture?
- What is the intended role of reflection, summaries, biographies, and other elements of e-portfolio design?
- What will ideal finished products look like, and what bodies of knowledge are they expected to represent?
- What exactly should portfolio owners bring to bear as evidence for their growth? Are particular media valued? Why?
- How will these expectations be communicated to instructors, students, and other participants?

Answering these questions meticulously prior to implementation and revisiting them regularly as the project matures paves the way for a successful project and a successful evaluation. Goals, strategies, and outcomes should be articulated early and tracked deliberately. If a project aims to use e-portfolios to support attainment of externally mandated achievement pressures (as is increasingly the case in public education environments), this articulated and logical framework is all the more important. If the logic model changes and evolves during the course of the project (a not uncommon occurrence), evaluation can document that growth as well and maintain a linked strategy for documenting impact.

EVALUATING E-PORTFOLIO STRATEGIES

In designing e-portfolio implementation, care should be taken to ensure that instructors provide clear and responsive technical and conceptual support for portfolio owners, illustrating precisely the nature of knowledge and learning that is to be generated and documented. In collecting and analyzing data to document strategies, researchers should consider both formal and informal channels and modes of support provided to e-portfolio owners. The role of peer mentoring, collaboration, and the use of external resources beyond those specifically dedicated to the portfolio program should be explored to understand best the types of support that prove most valuable and efficient to portfolio creators. To the extent possible, any gaps that can be identified between articulated or perceived needs for support and strategies to provide that support should be reported formatively and acted upon in successive generations of program improvement efforts.

EVALUATING E-PORTFOLIO OUTCOMES

Obtaining a standardized view of impact comparable across implementation contexts is especially challenging in the context of e-portfolios, as the richness and potential of the medium often creates transformative learning experiences that are unique to the individual portfolio creator at that moment in their personal and professional growth. Each of the three project examples discussed above generated a range of impact that in some ways defied easy categorization or causal linking. Consider some of the unexpected outcomes found in those e-portfolio uses:

- One portfolio user-advocate presented her own research showing improvement in attainment of professional growth goals for in-service students who used the PLP, both validating the merit of portfolio use and developing her own skills as research practitioner.
- One instructor charged with offering a course on e-portfolios was impressed enough with the experience that she persuaded her colleagues to collaborate with her in the development of a portfolio-based approach to their upcoming institutional accreditation.
- The visible success of a few portfolio users on a university faculty was cited in administrative and other meetings over the following year and influenced decisions made about budgets, hiring, planning, course syllabi, and program completion requirements.

Unexpected impacts are likely to comprise a powerful, perspective-enhancing set of outcomes in many e-portfolio implementation settings. In particular, the development and natural spread of innovative thinking and practices around assessment, technology, and collaboration surfaced in many settings that RMC studied. The following section presents lessons learned that may support researchers and practitioners in developing robust evaluation designs that capture the essence and power of e-portfolios for supporting the emergence of professional practice.

EVALUATION DESIGN

It is not practical here to catalog the abundant strategies and rules of thumb for effective research and evaluation that apply to e-portfolio projects and implementations. In general, the detailed evaluation research design should provide for explicit measurement of the link between project goals strategies, and outcomes on both formative and summative levels. Further, as with any research design, thoughtful and detailed design customization is critical. Effort placed into developing an evaluation customized to project goals and strategies pays off as evidence starts to accumulate. Many similar relevant generalizations exist. To limit the volume of this discussion while still retaining utility to the reader, only a few portfolio-specific principles for evaluation design are offered below.

RESEARCH QUESTIONS AND HYPOTHESES

Research questions to be answered and corresponding hypotheses to be tested form the core of research. All program evaluations should describe the basic correspondence between project goals and project outcomes, the influence of specific strategies for support, and the program's sustainability beyond the duration of funding. E-portfolio evaluators should aim to capture a detailed understanding of the complex intersection of technology proficiency, assessment literacy, and personal values and attitudes in alignment with their specific goals and intended outcomes. Measurement constructs tied to each then begin to suggest instrumentation and sampling strategies. For example, if instructors state that they hope students' e-portfolios will help them to get jobs, an effective evaluation partner can help explore the feasibility and desirability of hypothesis testing that can provide evidence of this link or its absence.

Focusing on a single desired area of impact undermines quality in the same way as would reliance on a single data source. In addition to missing the potential richness of unintended goals, strategies, or outcomes by program leaders, a proscribed focus on predetermined outcomes is unlikely to provide a full perspective on how e-portfolios and their users function in support of long term goals. Yet in the current environment of accountability it is reasonable to ask: what effects can be expected from investment in e-portfolios?

DATA COLLECTION, SAMPLING, AND INSTRUMENTATION

An effective data collection plan provides a body of evidence that can shed light on a phenomenon from different angles, triangulating multiple sources of evidence to support assertions about program intention (goals), activity (strategies), and impact (outcomes). An effective data collection plan for e-portfolio evaluation should address the full range of challenges that can accompany adoption of any complex technology. Different roles, levels of interest, and positions in the program logic model among stakeholders mean that the kinds of data they are best suited to provide varies. Focused sets of instrumentation help assure that research conclusions are both defensible and representative of the entire target population.

The strategy of best-practice sampling appeals to administrators looking to defend past and future funding decisions and highlight their successes, but alone such examples reveal little about the overall context of implementation. To balance and ground representation of program effectiveness, a random or census range of more typical examples among target populations is both more defensible and more likely to yield insights that will support formative improvement. All potentially impacted members of the intended program audience should be included in data collection, and any shortcomings in the availability of data should be acknowledged and explored. By complementing census sampling with site or exemplar nominations and screening, a few strong examples can illustrate the best potential of e-portfolios intended while also providing an accurate background of overall implementation.

Linkage between constructs that the portfolios are intended to measure and the data collection plan is of critical importance. But e-portfolios themselves are only the first and most obvious data sources in the effective study of an e-portfolio environment. If one wished to include, for example, the job-readiness question above in the evaluation design, data on local employers' attitudes and perceptions could complement student self-reports and employment demographic data to provide multiple points of triangulation allowing researchers to support their claims. Data collected regarding collaboration among stakeholders can illustrate the diffusion networks (Rogers, 1995) and relationships that support or impede program effectiveness. Other such process-oriented data might include how rubrics and criteria were developed and evolved, and the development and communication of expectations at multiple systemic levels.

Time plays another crucial role in the development of a body of evidence, whether contained in a research report or an e-portfolio. The complexity of knowledge adoption dictates that any evaluation study attempting to produce summative results within a single year will produce few if any results. Design should take into account the multiple layers of impact expected over several years of implementation; where this is impossible, researchers are forced to be extremely tentative in their assertions on all but a few primary levels of expected impact.

A note is warranted on the compatibility of e-portfolio research as described here with the publicly discussed "gold standard" clinical trial research methodology of random assignment to treatment and non-treatment conditions. Across the field of education, it seems evident that program funding decisions will be increasingly tied to more stringent definitions of quality research. However, a number of considerations make pure random assignment to portfolio and non-portfolio learning conditions a potentially misleading frame for research design. The limited scope of access to potential audience groups and the difficulty of measuring valued portfolio-based outcomes among portfolio nonusers both complicate a design stratified along those parameters. As with other technological innovations, the characteristics of users who embrace a portfolio methodology may hold important implications for their characteristics prior to portfolio use as compared to potential audience members who do not seek out active engagement with an e-portfolio as a learning tool. In other words, comparing volunteers and non-volunteers creates sample populations that already possess differing characteristics, confounding accurate measurement of how e-portfolio use influenced practice and performance. A matched comparison group strategy is more feasible in this case and controls for these previously existing differences between adopters and non-adopters. Implementations that do not initially serve their entire potential audience may be able to select participants from a pool of applicants randomly, creating matched comparison groups that are more likely to possess similar characteristics relevant to their portfolio use and its impact on their learning.

Naturally an evaluation design should take into account the full potential range of electronic artifacts that may comprise a given collection of e-portfolios. Ideally, specific criteria indicating mastery of practice should be evident in the electronic artifacts that the portfolio contains. Where this includes video of teaching performance, portfolio evaluation criteria should to the extent possible describe specific observable performances. Conceptual and technical expertise can be obtained by matching user self-ratings with quantified patterns in technical data where available. Technical portfolio systems themselves, whether off-the-shelf or highly customized, can often provide data on usage patterns that become meaningful in aggregate or through cross-tabulation with other development outcomes, such as hours logged, numbers of artifacts uploaded, or views of other users' e-portfolios. If candidates present or defend their portfolio to a group, these interactions provide yet further data relevant to expectations, comfort levels, and overall fluency of portfolio owners.

In general, evaluators should work to provide multiple data points broadly, creatively, and inclusively shedding light on different aspects of portfolio development and use. Short surveys can help clarify baselines and changes over time in users' perceptions of their access to the forms and documents that they need, their self-rated technical skills and challenges, and the usability of technology-based aspects of the e-portfolio development process.

ANALYTICAL FRAMES AND DATA ANALYSIS

Data collected and catalogued during earlier stages of research acquire meaning both from their natural patterns and the patterns into which researchers organize them. As potentially interesting and informative patterns become visible in the available data, researchers should keep in mind the relation of these new patterns and the originally posited research questions.

Formative data collection and reporting often can identify a number of dimensions to a given e-portfolio implementation that may not have been fully evident at the project's outset. At RMC Research, robust evaluation designs allowed our teams to incorporate these new concepts into later stages of data collection and analysis in multi-year studies. We were able to act quickly when information about the importance of certain lenses on change (in this case, cultural facilitation and group uses) began to percolate up from different settings. While the strength of the research base was limited by fewer years of data to draw on, the potential suggested of these new ideas about portfolios and cultural change nonetheless warranted their continued investigation. E-portfolio engagements come in many ranges of width and depth, and we hope that the field will embrace the importance of measures of success that recognize the full breadth and depth that lies in the power for educational growth and transformation.

EPISTEMOLOGY OF E-PORTFOLIO CONTENTS

Whether or not formative adjustments are available in the repertoire of tools for understanding the impact of an institution's e-portfolio use, data analysis will progress through various stages. Early among these will be cataloguing and coding of the contents, types of artifacts, included reflections, and other features that distinguish each portfolio example. To complement a pre-determined or a priori categorization list, understanding the meanings that e-portfolios have for their creators often will require evaluators to also incorporate emergent and natural patterns that occur in the set of portfolios under consideration.

Viewed philosophically, portfolio contents embody a range of epistemologies: a number of perspectives on what constitutes valid evidence that a given standard for excellence has been achieved. The strength of the coupling between evidence and standards will vary substantially. In our experience, instructors with more extensive experience in supporting their students through a portfolio process provided more specific criteria for evidence than did less "portfolio savvy" instructors. Further, technology database structures may support or constrain the way evidence and assertions are linked in a given e-portfolio structure. And naturally, the work products created by the students creating e-portfolios will show their own variation within the articulated epistemology, or required framing of evidence, that of the assigned portfolio structure. Even with clearly articulated guidelines, the content of e-portfolios can be difficult to analyze effectively. The nuances of learning and conceptual sophistication embedded in each portfolio usually vary substantially.

Accurately describing this variance within the delivered parameters is the primary analytical task involved in the evaluation of e-portfolios. A strong project will be framed from the outset in such a way that clear expectations and foundations in current research drive the conceptual intentions and practical execution of the given e-portfolio program. Several of the themes below proved useful in developing theoretical treatments for empirically validating the impacts of portfolios in educational improvement research. Continued attention to these themes should help contribute to the strong base of proven best practice in systemic application of portfolios and e-portfolio systems in education.

ASSESSMENT AND CULTURE: VALUES, ATTITUDES, AND PRACTICES

Used as institutional tools, portfolios can help organizations to develop, display, and share a common vision of assessment-driven thinking. Used and distributed across organizations, e-portfolios set the tone for developing and continuously improving the work highlighted through the portfolio. The widespread and shared practice of setting goals and reflecting on their attainment in a shared electronic environment can impact participants in subtle but powerful ways over time. Similarly, engaging in the process of reviewing and evaluating portfolios as a faculty member may influence the way individuals in that participating culture think about assessment. In institutions, this may bring up questions of personnel review and evaluation criteria, competing pressures with other forms of assessment, and the tension between assessments of learning and assessments for learning (cf. Shepard, 2000).

The argument is not academic. People in university settings we studied experienced in some cases a strong feeling that the learning purpose of e-portfolios was at odds with their role as accountability tools. In other settings, professors opined that teacher education students were getting turned off by the "hard sell" of portfolio work that was driven by pressure stemming from the National Council for Accreditation of Teacher Education. Describing the intense expectations around "filling an online box" related to mandated elements of teacher quality in state law, one participant feared that the e-portfolio was being used for "a checklist of competencies, not a tool for lifelong learning."

While institutional needs and pressures are real, the deeper benefits of e-portfolios accrue when they are used as tools for deep, ongoing, personally or institutionally meaningful learning. This type of learning is much harder to measure. E-portfolios make that task much easier, with structures that allow users to customize and employ supports of their own choosing, giving them flexibility and authenticity.

Data certainly can show that e-portfolios are engaging tools, approached by some users with deeply embedded learner motivation. However, the true gaps separating one e-portfolio from another may reflect an enormous range of institutional and socio-contextual issues.

INDIVIDUAL LEARNING

One line of e-portfolio evaluation inquiry explores individual impacts of e-portfolios on the learning experiences and other valued outcomes of students who assemble portfolios through these systems. While comfort and facility with technology is both a predictor and an outcome of e-portfolio use and satisfaction, a deeper understanding of user experiences will be enriched by considering a longer term view of how e-portfolios serve continued purposes in users' lives and careers. Compared to traditional portfolios, e-portfolios allow for a range and breadth of evidence showing mastery of desired outcomes that is virtually limitless. In the Project SABRE context, for example, video capture of teaching performance was seen by instructors as highly valuable. Prospective teachers, for their part, found the revealing nature of video captured teaching performance to be challenging and requiring a willingness to experience intense professional vulnerability. The transformation in attitudes of prospective teachers toward this experience consisted of one learning trajectory, while the dialogue around their actual teaching comprised another aspect of their learning experience.

Learner perceptions provide an important data source, and should be captured authentically, especially when doing so can influence future e-portfolio requirements. Good e-portfolio systems provide real evidence of mastery, and the mastery aimed for by each institution will best be reflected in its own faculty and student body. Research tools used to track changes in attitudes should be able to document the perceived value of and interest in e-portfolios compared to the perceived effort of creating them. Supports for learning and documentation of impact can both build from these basic adoption considerations.

As a static, moment-in-time collection of artifacts, an e-portfolio can show a learner's state of current ability in assigned areas. Alignment to taught content, interviews and syllabi, coherence of alignment and review criteria are but a few ways to capture time-segmented learning objectives. However, with the reflection component added to e-portfolio requirements, analysis becomes both richer and more complex. Reflecting on the setting and attainment of learning goals through an e-portfolio creates a more dynamic record over time, with multiple concrete artifacts illustrating a concrete developmental path. In some ways, the better the portfolio, the more personal the journey and the more difficult it is to quantify. The expertise represented in e-portfolios of the highest quality is growing, changing, and accelerating.

By consolidating and refining measures used by instructors to evaluate individual quality, researchers should be able to develop a coherent set of context-sensitive quality indicators using standard grounded analysis data reduction techniques and (e.g., Miles & Huberman, 1994). However, your data may reveal, for instance, a sensitive set of conditions for building on initial interest in portfolio technology that holds lessons for future support endeavors. Researchers should capture these insights related to individual learning trajectories if they are able.

INSTITUTIONAL LEARNING

A wide variety of frameworks and lenses are avaialble to consider institutional learning and organizational change in different settings (cf. Senge, Kleiner, Robers, Ross, Roth, & Smith, 1999; Argyris & Schön, 1996). In this important and often neglected context, cultural factors and attitudes about assessment, technology, and change have substantial impacts. Portfolios are shaped by guidelines for use and other official and unofficial culturally transmitted messages that instructors and institutions send to students about the importance and purposes of their e-portfolios. Those messages will also determine what forms of institutional learning around portfolios are likely to take place. Knowledge of the portfolio development process across institutions is still emergent in the literature, but the availability of data in the form of course syllabi, course content and requirements, budget allocations, and other sources do suggest frameworks for beginning to look beyond simple measures of adoption and integration into courses.

The clearest challenge to understanding systemic learning and e-portfolios is that systems themselves and the change they go through are complex and idiosyncratic. Issues of alignment across institutional initiatives, the role of adoption pressures and the position of e-portfolios as ancillary or central to the institutional mission, and the presence or absence of other reform efforts may all impact whether and how resources and attention go toward e-portfolios.

In an era of teacher performance expectations, teacher quality enhancement efforts, and teacher performance assessment, it is important to consider the deeper contextual reasons why an e-portfolio adoption has been embraced. Leadership or bottom-up pressures, the perceived advantages of e-portfolios compared to traditional systems, and other aspects driving a given e-portfolio engagement should be considered and measured as part of an evaluation that supports implementation goals.

As with most aspects of systemic implementation, a "cookie cutter" approach is less likely to be useful. At least a minimal unique set of indicators for system impact ought to be tailored to local use, and researchers should examine the context of goals and wider reform and renewal priorities in place at each institution. Other systemic factors that may impact a given implementation setting include institutional tradeoffs for money, technology, and human resources for support and training. The massive cultural and political systems around technology support and technology adoption certainly are not absent from e-portfolio implementation settings, nor is the obvious truth that that broken, error-prone, or otherwsise technically challenged implementaitons do not foster use. These and other barriers to implementation may provide important keys to the successes and failures of e-portfolio settings. Supports provided or created by the system, intentionally or unintentionally, may foster communication, collaboration, and social learning in ways that should be captured as well.

Finally, one of the most basic questions related to the implementation and use of e-portfolios involves whether or not their use is sustained over time. Changes in thinking, culture, and assessment practice usually become visible only after multiple years of iteration, design, and funding to accompany the e-portfolio structures and their use. Perhaps the final adopted version will look different than first envisioned, but even so, survival in a slightly different form is still survival. Sustainability of education technology systems is supported by a number of factors (cf. Billig, Sherry, & Havelock, 2005), and will look different from setting to setting depending on the supports for sustainability that are in place. In our experience, the reflection and growth in learning often had more durability than the funding, but the persistent ground-level and administrative advocates thus created held promise for the future.

LESSONS LEARNED

The challenges of evaluating, or documenting the impact, of e-portfolio systems and implementations goes hand in hand with the challenges of supporting their effective and engaged use. At RMC Research, we found that the most satisfying and worthwhile evaluation activities were those that were able to serve as accelerators for the quality and value of developed e-portfolios in each setting: when the formative evaluation reporting we provided illuminated a pathway for better and more successful implementations. In any setting, evaluators should make sure to gain access to external perspectives and expertise in program evaluation in order to capture as thoroughly as possible the complex intersection of institutions, individuals, technology, assessment, and learning that e-portfolios represent. In a professional culture that increasingly values documentation of results, plans to evaluate should be thoughtfully linked to a range of possible measures that can capture a range of effective and inspiring potential learning outcomes.

Our most substantial frustrations as evaluators emerged from settings where leaders did not deeply consider the importance of customizing e-portfolio systems, the nature of performances expected and required, or the ways that quality of portfolio products would be scored and evaluated. In creating e-portfolio implementation designs, program leaders should collaborate with evaluators to ensure that the results generated by a given program document worthwhile and important growth that occurs in portfolio use. They should balance a simple system for assuring inter-rater reliability with sensitivity to the full complexity of learning outcomes that the e-portfolio is meant to support. External perspectives can help program advocates recognize and strike a balance between potentially competing purposes.

Most e-portfolio implementations in higher education are intended to serve a range of outcomes, in which student demonstration of core teaching competencies may be secondary to program accreditation pressures, institutional pressures for technology integration, and other factors. An effective evaluation should document the full range of tradeoffs, intended and actual uses, perceptions of purpose and utility, and learning outcomes associated with the use of a given e-portfolio system in context. The match between an e-portfolio structure and the culture in which it is meant to be used is a critical aspect of implementation, and in our experience e-portfolios have their most profound impact when they serve to initiate, catalyze, or illustrate institutional cultural change.

Portfolio implementation is a journey in which individuals over time define what they are trying to accomplish. Yet practical considerations often undermine the potential of e-portfolios, and must be addressed thoroughly in order for implementations to flourish. Technical support, infrastructure, and expertise working with technology environments will all influence e-portfolio results. While increases in technology proficiency across different levels of society may see technology proficiency fade over time as a barrier to implementation, other learning curves related to assessment and the use of evidence are likely to continue challenging users in their initial and extended engagements with e-portfolios. Identifying those complementary proficiencies should suggest further key supports for implementation to help faculty and students develop their work in assessment, technology, collaboration, standards, content, and school improvement. In a given situation, program leaders, advocates, and researchers will need to select a subset of areas for focused improvement while also building on existing strengths.

IMPLICATIONS OF AUTHENTIC ASSESSMENT FOR HIGH-STAKES ACCOUNTABILITY SYSTEMS

- Cyclical improvement in portfolio quality accompanied the sustained use of e-portfolio systems in most every setting where RMC Research served as evaluators. However, documenting that quality in ways that fulfill high-stakes accountability needs can prove extremely challenging. To engage with the issue honestly and deeply, planners and evaluators should consider how realistically their portfolio guidelines support engagement with the essential dilemmas and central questions of its discipline. By carefully translating these concerns to measurable outcomes and providing aligned support for the e-portfolio development process, e-portfolios can provide deep and authentic evidence that accountability imperatives are being addressed and met.
- Distinguishing impacts on individual students and on institutions and where they meet requires careful assessment of each audience as a documented part of the portfolio implementation design accompanied by a logic model or theory of change illustrating the thinking behind how the implementers intend to obtain their chosen results. The vision connecting high-stakes mandates with complex and authentic evidence illustrating their attainment must be embraced, articulated, and advocated by committed leaders and innovators who believe in the potential of e-portfolios to support

deep and meaningful attainment of all kinds of learning goals and outcomes.

CONCLUSION: DIRECTIONS IN EVALUATING THE IMPACT OF E-PORTFOLIO SYSTEMS

Authentically understanding e-portfolios means understanding how technology, assessment, institutional culture, and the art and science of learning intersect to provide a platform for developing a thorough and thoughtfully constructed body of evidence that portrays growth in knowledge and skills. Electronic facilitators for communicating about learning activities and outcomes and capturing permanent records of detailed practice through video make e-portfolios at once more complex and more powerful as tools for documenting and supporting learning gains concretely. As technologies in the field mature and stabilize, we hope to see further growth and availability of simple and powerful tools for collecting, organizing, presenting, and making meaning of information about learning and student achievement in its many forms.

Until a deeply reflective approach to assessment and the use of data to illustrate competence become deeply integrated and embedded in the institutional and personal practice of educators, the true impact of e-portfolios may remain too new a tale to tell. However, effective research methods can certainly document early steps taken toward connecting learning and its documentation in deeply meaningful ways. By connecting implementation activities and supports to the quality, depth, impacts, and uses of e-portfolio products, formative and summative program evaluation can play a valuable role in supporting best practices in e-portfolio assessment across systemic levels.

Technology use and assessment accountability are increasingly norms in our society. As the practices of technology use become integrated with a cohesive, assessment-oriented response to accountability pressures, many school and university systems and partnerships we saw were pushing toward systemic fruition of a deeply meaningful vision of e-portfolio use.

Contemporary pressure in the educational data tool industries still favors a compliance perspective on high-stakes accountability measures. Assessment for learning (Shepard, 2000) was less common than a testing glut and corresponding emphasis on direct instruction of discrete reading and math skills. Multiple tiers of systematic data collection and analysis were increasingly available in such toolsets, but few systems provided support for making meaningful connections with included technological records of qualitative data. Those that did were engaging, developing and reliably using rubrics, common assessments, and forms of discussion and mentoring to use a detailed qualitative body of evidence about student growth (Light, Wexler, & Heinze, 2005). Parallel pressures in higher education are working to deconstruct, quantify, and prescribe teacher accountability (cf. Coble, Edelfelt, & Kettlewell, 2004). Point-in-time, high-stakes assessments were still prevalent in many settings, and e-portfolios were often embraced in these settings as a way to demonstrate rigorous adherence to new standards.

Acting on some levels independently of their mandated intentions, the highest-impact uses of e-portfolios encountered by RMC Research still tended to be individual in nature. Advocates continued to build positive momentum in pockets of innovation where teacher-oriented and student-focused development and uses of assessment tools prevailed. However, the complex, messy, and authentic learning power of technology-supported portfolio assessment was often secondary to prescriptive and simplistic uses of e-portfolios for specific assessment ends. In some settings, we saw advocates sharing their concerns with decision makers at all levels of the system, while in other settings they continued their individual journeys with sporadic or nonexistent support.

Continuing and effective integration of research, practice, and industry will be required to provide the intuitive, usable, customizable, powerful, and affordable open-source tools for collecting, analyzing, and presenting a broad range of quantitative and qualitative assessment data. E-portfolio advocates will need to continue emphasizing explicit linkage to and reflection on educational goals, building support for a portfolio-based model of academic and professional improvement and assessment. Widespread use of such technologies will, over time, create large samples of active users and provide data that can be analyzed to discern long-term impacts systematically on individuals and institutions. Evaluators, professors, graduate students, and action researchers based in and out of schools, classrooms, and universities can become aware of and document the pressures and considerations shaping their own initial steps and suggest effective measures for supporting long-term proliferation along dimensions they identify. By designing research that captures the multiple layers of potential impact and the factors that mitigate and influence implementation, a detailed portrait of implementation can be developed that supports transformative assessment practices.

It seems a reasonable hope that continuing cycles of site-based advocacy and improvement will, over time, begin to provide a continuous record of the positive impacts of widespread and sustained e-portfolio use. Many implementations will stall, fail, or fall prey to competing pressures before such a continuous record is evident. Settings where high-quality e-portfolios persist are certain to provide a tale worth telling. With effective evaluation built into their implementations, leaders advocating the generation and use of new and powerful forms of assessment data and reflection can ensure that their evaluation story displays the value of their work both thoroughly and persuasively.

REFERENCES

Argyris, C., & Schön, D. A. (1996). *Organizational learning II: Theory, method, and practice.* New York: Addison-Wesley.

Barrett, H. (2005) *Digital storytelling in electronic portfolios: Using reflection on experience to improve learning for K–12 students and teacher professional development.* Breakout session: International Reading Association, San Antonio, TX, May 3, 2005.

Billig, S., Sherry, L., & Havelock, B. (2005). Challenge 98: Sustaining the work of a regional technology integration initiative. *British Journal of Educational Technology, 36*(6), 987–1003

Chen, H. (Ed.)(2004). Practical program evaluation: Assessing and improving planning, implementation, and effectiveness. Thousand Oaks, CA: Sage.

Coble, C., Edelfelt, R., & Kettlewell, J. (2004). *Who's in charge here? The changing landscape of teacher preparation in America.* Denver, CO: Education Comission of the States.

Cooksy, L., Gill, P., & Kelly, P. A. (2001). The Program Logic Model as an Integrative Framework for a Multimethod Evaluation. *Evaluation and Program Planning, 24*(2), 109–28.

Havelock, B., Gibson, D., & Sherry, L. (2003). The Personal Learning Planner: Collaboration through online learning and publication. In *Proceedings of society for information technology and teacher education international conference 2003* (pp. 3590–3597). Norfolk, VA: AACE.

Havelock, B., & Sherry, L. (2003). *p2/t3 PT3 Grant, Year 2 Evaluation.* CSU San Bernardino: RMC Research.

Hiebert, J., Gallimore, R., & Stigler, J. W. (2002) A knowledge base for the teaching profession: What would it look like, and how can we get one? *Educational Researcher, 31*(5), 3–15.

Light, D., Wexler, D., & Heinze, C. (2005, March). *Keeping teachers in the center: A framework of data-driven decision making.* Paper presented at the Society for Information Technology and Teacher Education (SITE) Conference, Phoenix, AZ.

McLaughlin, J., & Jordan, G. (1999). Logic models: A tool for telling your program's performance story. *Evaluation Program Planning, 22,* 65–72.

Miles, M., & Huberman, M. (1994) *Qualitative data analysis (2nd edition).* Thousand Oaks, CA: Sage.

Rogers, E. (1995). *Diffusion of innovations* (4th ed.). New York: Free Press.

Senge, P., Kleiner, A., Roberts, C., Ross, R., Roth, G., & Smith, B. (1999). *The dance of change: The challenges of sustaining momentum in learning organizations.* New York: Currency Doubleday.

Shepard, L. (2000). The role of assessment in a learning culture. *Educational Researcher, 29*(7), 4–14.

Sherry, L. (2004). *TALENT: Final Report.* Portsmouth, NH: RMC Research.

Sherry, L. (2005). *p2/t3 PT3 Grant: Final Evaluation.* CSU San Bernardino: RMC Research.

Sherry, L., Havelock, B., & Gibson, D. (2004). The Personal Learning Planner: An online environment for mentoring, collaboration, and publication. In T. Roberts (Ed.), *Computer-supported collaborative learning in higher education,* (pp. 201–217). Hershey, PA: Idea Group Publishing.

Weiss, H., Coffman, J., & Bohan-Baker, M. (2002, Dec. 5–6). *Evaluation's role in supporting initiative sustainability.* Paper prepared for the fifth biannual meeting of the Urban Seminar Series on Children's Health and Safety. Cambridge, MA: Harvard University.

Zhao, Y., & Frank, K. (2003). Factors affecting technology uses in schools: An ecological perspective. *American Educational Research Journal, 40*(4), 807–840.

NOTE

1. PLP is not a pseudonym. See also Havelock, Gibson & Sherry (2003); Sherry, Havelock, & Gibson (2004); or http://www.learningcentral.org/ for more information.

CHAPTER 5

WEB-BASED DIGITAL TEACHING PORTFOLIOS

What Happens After They Graduate?

Natalie B. Milman
The George Washington University

INTRODUCTION

Many teacher educators in schools, colleges, and departments of education (SCDEs) have been expanding their views about how they might measure teacher competence and knowledge. Traditionally, measures only involved the use of standardized approaches (i.e., NTE, PRAXIS exams). However, today, more and more SCDEs are also using authentic measures such as teaching portfolios (Wray, 2001) to provide more information about a teacher's ability to teach. A teaching portfolio, according to Shulman (1998), is the "structured documentary history of a set of coached or mentored acts of teaching, substantiated by samples of student portfolios, and fully realized only through reflective writing, deliberation, and conversation" (p. 37). McKinney (1998) suggests that "[teacher] educators have found that well-constructed portfolios may help to capture the complexities of learning, teaching, and learning to teach when used as authentic

Evaluating Electronic Portfolios in Teacher Education, pages 91–109

assessment tools within courses and programs in Colleges of Education" (p. 85). Moreover, three professional associations representing the "three-legged stool of teacher quality" (National Commission on Teaching and America's Future, 1996, p. 29), the Interstate New Teacher Assessment and Support Consortium (INTASC), the National Board for Professional Teaching Standards (NBPTS), and the National Council for Accreditation of Teacher Education (NCATE) advocate the use of teaching portfolios as performance-based measures.

Many teacher educators in SCDEs have been exploring and implementing the creation of digital teaching portfolios by preservice teachers for varied and sometimes conflicting purposes (e.g., to meet NCATE requirements) (Strudler & Wetzel, 2005). Digital teaching portfolios (DTP's), sometimes referred to as multimedia portfolios, electronic portfolios, e-folios, webfolios, and electronically-augmented portfolios, are similar to traditional teaching portfolios in content but present professional materials in digital format. Throughout this paper, "digital teaching portfolios" may also be referred to as "electronic teaching portfolios"—they refer to the same type of portfolio. Professional materials included in DTPs are presented using a combination of digital or electronic media such as audio recordings, hypermedia programs, database, spreadsheet, video, and word processing software.

The use of DTPs supports current reform efforts by many SCDEs that have been focusing on the need to prepare preservice teachers to use technology better. Reports by the American Council on Education, (1999), the CEO Forum of Educational Technology, (1999), the International Society for Technology in Education (1999), NCATE, (1997), Persichitte, Tharp, and Caffarella (1996), the U.S. Congress Office of Technology and Assessment (1995), and Willis and Mehlinger (1996) have all suggested that SCDEs are not adequately preparing preservice teachers to use technology. Digital teaching portfolios provide SCDEs with an authentic and purposeful strategy for preparing preservice teachers to use technology (Milman, 1999, 2000; Kilbane & Milman, 2003).

REVIEW OF RELEVANT LITERATURE

A considerable amount of research has emerged on the topic of teaching portfolios in recent years. Several studies suggest that teaching portfolios promote reflective thinking and practice (Borko, Michalec, Timmons, & Siddle, 1997; Dietz, 1995; Jackson, 1998; Loughran & Corrigan, 1995; Lyons, 1998a, 1998b; Stroble, 1995; Wade & Yarbrough, 1996), professional knowledge development (Mokhtari, Yellin, Bull, & Montgomery,1996; Zidon, 1996), and professional growth (Dietz, 1995; Green & Smyser, 1996;

Wray, 2001). Others contend (Barrett, 1999, 2000; Kilbane & Milman, 2003; McKinney, 1998; Milman, 1999, 2000) that the creation of DTPs by preservice teachers can result in teachers who are confident in their abilities as educators and in their use and application of technology. Research on DTPs has focused on preservice teachers' experiences constructing such portfolios, but not on the role of DTPs in their professional development and teaching practice beyond their preservice experience.

Digital teaching portfolios can act as springboards for teachers' professional development in several ways (Kilbane & Milman, 2003). Since DTP's are biographical accounts of teachers' work, they provide snapshots of teachers' competence during set periods in time. Teachers can review and reflect on their work by examining their past, present, and future goals for improvement. They also can reevaluate their beliefs and philosophies to see how they have grown both professionally and philosophically. Moreover, teachers can create DTPs that include a plan for professional development—and as time progresses, they can see if they have achieved these goals. Finally, by examining portfolios both teachers and other personnel (such as a principal) can help determine teachers' needs for additional professional growth and ways to achieve it.

This chapter presents the results of a mixed method study to examine the role of DTPs in teachers' employment and classroom practices since they graduated. It also examines teacher beliefs about portfolios and describes decisions made regarding the research design (discussed in the methods section of this chapter). The purpose of the study was to learn:

1. What role, if any, did the DTPs play in gaining employment?
2. How have teachers applied the technology skills learned in creating their DTPs to classroom teaching, if at all?
3. Which factors promoted or hindered modifying, updating, and/or maintaining the DTPs?
4. What were the teachers' beliefs about the value of DTPs for preservice and/or inservice teachers?

METHODS

The researcher determined the research design by applying a typology (see Figure 5.1). This typology illustrates the decisions the researcher made for this study, as well as the process for making those decisions. As Figure 5.1 shows, the first step in this process involved examining the purpose of the study through the lens (researcher biases and experiences) of the researcher. This was done while simultaneously weighing the theoretical framework and literature about the topic of portfolios which framed the questions and

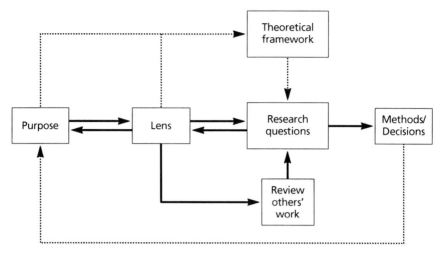

Figure 5.1 Typology for this study (Newman, Ridenour, Newman, & DeMarco, 2003, p. 174).

in turn informed the researcher's purpose and focus of study. Although this process appears linear, it is not. It is a recursive, non-linear process that resulted in using a sequential mixed method design.

SEQUENTIAL MIXED METHOD DESIGN

This study employed a sequential mixed method design (Tashakkori & Teddlie, 1998). Mixed method studies include:

> the collection or analysis of both quantitative and/or qualitative data in a single study in which the data are collected concurrently or sequentially, are given a priority, and involve the integration of the data at one or more stages in the process of research. (Cresswell, Plano Clark, Gutmann, & Hanson, 2003, p. 212)

Sequential mixed method design studies, which fall under the mixed method umbrella, consist of two methods that occur in different phases of a study, each applying *different* methods, and conducted sequentially. Often one phase is completed prior to the subsequent phase. For this study, the quantitative phase was completed prior to the qualitative one.

A number of factors contributed to the decision for utilizing the "QUAN → qual" design (Morse, 2003, p. 198). First, one must understand that there are a number of purposes for conducting mixed method research in addition to the typical elements that influence the design of a study (e.g., theoretical framework, research questions, phenomenon under investigation). They are:

1. triangulation or seeking convergence of results;
2. complementarity, or examining overlapping and different facets of a phenomenon;
3. initiation, or discovering paradoxes, contradictions, fresh perspectives;
4. development, or using the methods sequentially, such that results from the first method inform the use of the second method; and
5. expansion, or mixed methods adding breadth and scope to a project. (Greene, Caracelli, & Graham, 1989, as cited in Tashakkori & Teddlie, 1998, p. 43)

Thus, the reasons for utilizing this design were for the qualitative portion of the study to:

1. triangulate data collected and support convergence of results from data collected initially via the questionnaire
2. complement items examined in the questionnaire and provide further convergence of findings
3. initiate new findings or questions to examine as a result of the findings from the questionnaire
4. develop further the findings from the questionnaire—the findings of the questionnaire were used to develop the questions utilized in the qualitative interview
5. expand upon the findings of the questionnaire by providing more depth and breadth.

Other reasons for utilizing this method were that mixed methods research: (a) helps researchers examine and answer questions that other methodologies cannot, (b) provides a stronger basis for making conclusions, and (c) illustrates findings using different views (Teddlie & Tashakkori, 2003). In this study, these were all factors that influenced the decision to apply a mixed method design.

Since several of the researcher's questions could be answered best using a survey, a quantitative questionnaire was designed to answer those questions. Yet, it was clear when designing the study that all of the questions could not be adequately answered using the questionnaire. Therefore, the researcher decided to include a few open-ended questions at the end of the questionnaire and also to conduct phone interviews with a "convenience sample" (Kemper, Stringfield, & Teddlie, 2003, p. 280) of the participants for purposes of triangulation, complementarity, and most importantly, expansion of findings. Because all of the participants did not agree to participate in a phone interview, the sample for the interviews consisted of those willing to participate—which was five of the participants. A benefit of this design was that the researcher was able to craft questions based on the participants' responses to the questionnaire; therefore, questions were focused on the research questions and any gaps in examining them that the survey could not answer.

Course context. Electronic Teaching Portfolios was an elective, one-credit, pilot preservice teacher education course offered during the spring semesters of 1998, 1999, and 2000 at a mid-Atlantic public university. The school of education in this university offers a five-year teacher education program in which students earn a bachelor's degree in an academic major, as well as a Masters in Teaching. The objectives of the course were for students to create teaching portfolios that were published on the World Wide Web using the Interstate New Teacher Assessment and Support Consortium's (INTASC) *Model Standards for Beginning Teachers* (Darling-Hammond, 1992) as a framework, to reflect upon their coursework and teaching experiences, and to become more proficient in the use of technology.

The course met once a week for an hour, followed by an hour of open lab time in which the instructors were available to help students individually. In 1998, the class was taught in a multimedia laboratory comprised primarily of PowerMac Macintosh computers. In subsequent years, the course was taught in a PC lab. The website development software used to create the portfolios were Claris HomePage in 1998 and Macromedia Dreamweaver in 1999 and 2000; these programs were chosen because of their availability in the laboratories in which the courses were taught. In the lab, students had access to their own computer, as well as digital cameras, scanners, and the Internet.

In the course, students learned how to develop a web-based teaching portfolio, write reflective statements, and critique each other's work. They also learned how to convert files, as well as how to design, organize, and present the components of the portfolio in a series of linked web pages. A topic for one of the class sessions was ways in which the participants might update and maintain their portfolios after they graduated with the hope that they would continue to use the portfolios as long-term professional development tools.

Participants. The participants in this study were 20 of 30 former preservice teacher education students enrolled in the graduate education program at a mid-Atlantic public university. Each one had participated in an elective, one-credit course, *Electronic Teaching Portfolios*, during the spring semester of 1998, 1999, or 2000. All but three had graduated in the same semester in which they took the course (they graduated the subsequent year). Participants completed the course in different years: Six completed the course in 1998, nine in 1999, and five in 2000.

Of the 20 participants, 17 were practicing inservice teachers (eight elementary, four middle, and six high school) at the time of the study. Two other participants had taught only one year and were enrolled in postgraduate programs (one of which was in a graduate Ph.D. program of instructional technology, the other in Rabbinical School). One participant chose to become a university level career counselor rather than a teacher although she had been offered a teaching position upon graduation. All but one (the career counselor) of the participants had a minimum of one year of teaching experience. The practicing teachers were teaching in several states: California (2), Connecticut (2), Georgia (1), New Jersey (2), New York (1), Ohio, (1), South Carolina (1), and Virginia (6). Also, one was teaching in Switzerland.

Data sources and analyses. Erickson's (1986) approach to data analysis, analytic induction, was utilized throughout this study. Analytic induction calls for the generation of empirical assertions which are then warranted through a search for instances of confirming or disconfirming evidence. Through the analyses of data and the questions that originated the study, a set of empirical assertions were formulated and warranted through a search of confirming and disconfirming evidence from the quantitative and qualitative data collected and analyzed. As assertions were formulated, the corpus of data was reviewed continuously to verify the validity of the empirical warrants. Discrepant case analysis was used to confirm or disconfirm the empirical assertions as they were formed. Four assertions were warranted through analyses of the quantitative and qualitative data. The assertions are presented in the findings section using exemplars from both the quantitative and qualitative data.

Quantitative methods involved the mailing of a questionnaire to 23 former preservice teacher education students (contact information was not available for 7 of the former 30 students) who had participated in the course, *Electronic Teaching Portfolios.* Twenty questionnaires (a return rate of 87%) were completed and returned with signed informed consent forms. The questionnaire consisted of 52 items clustered into the following categories: Background, access, use of technology, (beliefs about) electronic teaching portfolios, and barriers (to updating and maintaining portfolios). The majority of the items on the questionnaire required responses using a 4- or 5-point Likert scale format. Quantitative data were analyzed and reported using descriptive statistics in support of the empirical assertions formulated.

Qualitative methods included comments written in an open-ended section of the questionnaire and phone interviews conducted with five of the participants (this was a convenience sample–these were the only participants who agreed to participate in an interview). Phone interviews, ranging between 30 and 60 minutes, were taped, transcribed, and analyzed using analytic induction.

FINDINGS

Analyses of the data revealed that the participants found their DTPs useful in the employment process and in learning technology skills that were later applied in their teaching. All of the participants valued creating their DTPs, most also responded that they believed that preservice and inservice teachers should develop DTPs. Yet, the majority had not updated their DTPs. Several systemic conditions (e.g., lack of time, support, and incentives, as well as curricular demands) acted as barriers to maintaining and updating their DTPs after graduation. These findings are described below. Table 5.1 outlines the series of assertions that were warranted through analytic induction.

Assertion 1: Digital teaching portfolios were useful, but not always pivotal in gaining employment.

Digital teaching portfolios were useful to the participants of the study in gaining employment for several reasons. First and foremost, the participants believed they were well prepared to tackle any questions asked during interviews because they had spent countless hours reflecting on their work, educational philosophy, and student teaching experiences. Also, because they had spent so much time reviewing their work, they could provide concrete answers to the questions asked by interviewers. A few had even included items in their portfolios that they were asked to address in many of their applications. They noted that having created portfolios helped them prepare for their interviews—they were more confident in the whole inter-

---

TABLE 5.1 Empirical Assertions

1. Digital teaching portfolios were useful, but not always pivotal in gaining employment.
2. Most teachers applied the technology skills learned from developing DTPs as preservice teachers with the exception of Web site design skills.
3. Teachers had positive beliefs about DTPs, even years after creating their own as preservice teachers.
4. Systemic, external conditions acted as barriers to the teachers' implementation of DTPs and technology in general.

view process. Also, several applicants described having sent out cover letters that included the URL (web site address) to their DTPs.

The DTPs, however, did not play a pivotal role in the employment of the majority of the participants in the study. When asked to respond to the following statement, "I believe my electronic teaching portfolio played a role in my gaining employment," 40% responded that their portfolios did play a role (10% "strongly agree," 30% "agree") and 60% responded that they did not believe they had played a role at all (15% selected "strongly disagree," 45% "disagree"). One participant shared the following:

> I found that there was little interest by interviewers to take the time to look up my electronic résumé. I had a paper copy of the main pages to show interviewers, and they seemed impressed by my abilities and knowledge. (questionnaire, participant #22)

Although the majority of participants did not believe that their DTPs were the primary reasons for receiving job offers, several participants said or wrote that they believed their portfolios were impressive tools that did play an important role in securing employment, as one participant wrote:

> When I applied for a job, my school called me for a phone interview. At the end of the interview the principal said he was impressed and would like to see my résumé. The job depended on my classes and grades. I told him that I would send it, but it would be faster if he pulled it up off of my electronic portfolio. The next day they called offering me the job. They were so impressed with the electronic portfolio. I know it was the reason I got the job so quickly! (questionnaire, participant #9)

Also, another participant expressed the same sentiment in a phone interview:

> I'm really glad I created one [a digital teaching portfolio]. It was a very impressive tool during my interviews. The principal thought I was really techno-savvy! And now that I have served on interviewing committees, I know why they were impressed. No one else has walked through our doors with an electronic portfolio like mine. (interview, participant #17)

These data illustrate that the creation of DTPs played a role in helping the teachers who participated in this study gain employment—whether it was preparing the teacher candidates to tackle the questions asked during interviews or as impressive tools of their technology prowess and teaching knowledge and ability. However, the data also show that the role was not a pronounced one in gaining employment.

Assertion 2: Most teachers applied the technology skills learned from developing dtps as preservice teachers with the exception of web site design skills.

The majority of participants in this study indicated that they had applied the skills learned in developing their DTPs in their teaching and/or professional activities, with the exception of web site design skills. In the questionnaire, when asked to rate their response to the statement, "I have applied technology skills learned in developing my electronic teaching portfolio in my teaching and/or other professional activities," 25% of the participants selected "strongly agree," 45% "agree," 25% "disagree" and 5% "strongly disagree."

Another section of the questionnaire focused on the use of technology to ascertain the types of computer technologies teachers were using for classroom instruction. Participants were asked to rate (on a scale of 1 = "never," 2 = "infrequently," 3 = "sometimes," 4 = "often," and 5 = "very often") how often they used computers in their classrooms for a variety of purposes. Participants reported using them in a number of ways, as Table 5.2 demonstrates.

As Table 5.2 shows, the types of applications that participants used most often were word processing, accessing the World Wide Web, email, and research. Computers were least used for multimedia and Web site development.

Most of the participants in the 1998 and 1999 courses had not had any experience creating web sites prior to creating their DTPs as teacher candidates (Milman, 1999, 2000). Even though web site creation was a skill learned in developing their DTPs, 80% of the participants replied that they

TABLE 5.2 Use of Technology in the Classroom (N = 19)

	M	SD
Educational games and simulations	2.95	1.13
Presentation tools (powerpoint /slideshows)	2.74	1.41
Multimedia development (i.e., hyperstudio, macromedia director)	1.89	1.15
Research	4.05	.71
Wordprocessing	4.58	.69
Desktop publishing (i.e., brochures, newsletters)	3.32	1.53
Email	4.79	.42
World wide web access	4.58	.61
Web page development	1.95	1.35
Whole class instruction	2.68	1.34
Data collection and analysis	2.42	1.35

had not taught their own students how to develop web pages. On the other hand, 15% reported having taught their students these skills (two students, 5%, did not answer the question). These findings are exemplified in the following comments, "I have incorporated almost all of the technology we learned in the [DTP] class in my teaching but I have not used web page building" (interview, participant #17). Further, the following section reveals that participants' confidence in creating and teaching their own students to create web sites was low. Teachers learned many technology skills while developing their DTPs as preservice teachers. However, of these skills, multimedia and web page development were the ones that transferred the least to their classroom teaching.

Assertion 3: Teachers held positive beliefs about DTPs, even years after creating their own as preservice teachers

Several questionnaire items addressed participants' beliefs about the benefits of creating DTPs (see Table 5.3), as well as whether or not they thought preservice and inservice teachers should create traditional and/or DTPs. Also, two separate items were geared to learning whether participants believed teacher education programs should incorporate traditional and/or electronic teaching portfolios into their programs. For these items, participants were asked to rate their level of agreement with a statement on a scale of one to four (1 = "strongly disagree," 2 = "disagree," 3 = "agree," or 4 = "strongly agree").

TABLE 5.3   Beliefs About Digital Teaching Portfolios (N = 20)

	M	SD
I believe all preservice teachers should develop a teaching portfolio	3.50	.76
I believe all inservice teachers should develop a teaching portfolio	3.20	9.41
I believe all preservice teachers should develop an electronic teaching portfolio	3.10	.72
I believe all inservice teachers should develop an electronic teaching portfolio	2.90	.97
Teaching portfolios should be incorporated into all teacher education programs	3.30	.73
Electronic teaching portfolios should be incorporated into all teacher education programs	3.30	.47
I believe teachers should receive incentives (i.e., training, stipends) for developing and maintaining electronic teaching portfolios	3.35	.75

All of the participants responded that they had benefited from creating a DTP (65% strongly agree, 35% agree). In one interview, one participant reflected on the benefits of her teaching portfolio:

> I very much enjoyed creating my electronic teaching portfolio during my pre-service teacher training. It helped me to focus on my teaching philosophy, my teaching experiences, and my goals for the future. I think all teachers should have the opportunity to create an electronic teaching portfolio using appropriate technology. (interview, participant #21)

Another participant noted a similar sentiment about creating her portfolio:

> I believe that electronic teaching portfolios offer some very compelling benefits: such a portfolio requires that a teacher organize a body of work and reflect upon its educational importance, other teachers can review this work (lessons, etc....) on the Internet and perhaps use some ideas in their own classrooms, potential employers can learn a lot about a teacher's interests and strengths, and parents can use this site as a source of information both about the teacher and the learning their child explores in the classroom. (questionnaire, participant #12)

The quantitative and the qualitative data show that the participants believed that creating DTPs was a positive experience. There were two items on the questionnaire that asked participants to rate themselves on a scale of one to four (1 = "strongly disagree," 2 = "disagree," 3 = "agree," or 4 = "strongly agree") to describe the degree to which they agreed or disagreed with the following statements:

- I am confident creating Web sites (25% strongly disagree, 40% disagree, 25% agree, 10% strongly agree)
- I am confident teaching students to create Web sites (45% strongly disagree, 25% disagree, 20% agree, 10% strongly agree)

In general, teachers reported having positive beliefs about the use of DTPs for preservice and inservice teachers. In fact, the majority of the participants indicated in the questionnaire and/or the interview that they benefited a great deal from the creation of their DTPs.

Assertion 4: Systemic, external conditions acted as barriers to the teachers' implementation of DTPs and technology in general

All of the participants in this study, except for one, expressed a desire to update and maintain their DTPs. However, of all the participants, only one was working on updating her DTP although she had not uploaded her portfolio because she did not remember how (she was updating her portfolio from a version she had saved on a floppy disk). Two other teachers were required to maintain print-based portfolios for certification purposes by the state in which they were teaching (Connecticut). Yet, it was unclear whether state officials would accept a DTP, as one of these teachers explained: "I would love it if we had the option to create our required portfolio electronically instead of on paper, but I don't believe it's possible" (questionnaire, participant #3).

One section of the questionnaire focused on barriers (see Table 5.4) to updating and maintaining portfolios. This section included seven Likert-style items ranging from 1 = "never a barrier" to 4 = "often a barrier." The most significant barrier to updating and maintaining a DTP was the lack of time ($M = 3.60$, $SD = .75$). Lack of incentives and knowledge about how to update and upload their portfolios also were perceived to be barriers by the participants.

When asked why they had not taught their own students to develop web sites, participants cited a lack of time, support, and confidence as reasons why they had not. In an interview, one participant even said that she wished that the former instructors of the course could work with her at her school.

TABLE 5.4 Barriers to Updating and Maintaining Digital Teaching Portfolios ($N = 20$)

	M	SD
Lack skills	2.50	.95
Lack of equipment or access to equipment	2.60	.88
Lack of time to update or maintain one	3.60	.75
Lack of Internet access	1.40	.60
Lack of knowledge about how to update my site	2.95	1.00
Lack of knowledge about how to upload my site elsewhere	2.90	1.07
Lack of incentives to maintain site	2.89	.87

More realistically, however, she noted that she probably would do a better job of integrating technology into her classroom instruction if there was a technology coordinator at her school to help her, but her school did not have someone with such expertise.

Through analyses of phone interviews and the open-ended section of the questionnaire, other systemic barriers became clear. There was inadequate time, resources, and support available to teachers for implementing DTPs. Moreover, the pressures of day-to-day teaching responsibilities and demands (such as a standards-based curriculum) were significant barriers to maintaining and updating the DTPs, as one participant wrote:

I would love to redevelop my portfolio, but in a standards-driven environment I have time for little else. Similarly, I must meet so many standards and have only one school provided classroom computer that is current enough to handle Windows 98. (questionnaire, participant #25).

Another participant wrote that she experienced other barriers:

The main obstacles I face in updating my own electronic teaching portfolio is the lack of access to updated Web creation software resources, lack of technical knowledge about how to link all the pages together, and how to upload my site on a server. It would be easier to maintain my portfolio if I had more time and incentives offered by my school district. (questionnaire, participant #21)

Systemic conditions such as time, limited resources, and curricular constraints (standards) acted as barriers to the implementation of DTPs by the participants in this study.

DISCUSSION

The participants in this study indicated that they found the creation of DTP's to be beneficial—but not critical—in gaining employment. Whether it was having a DTP or the speed with which the principal could access the teachers' DTPs that was the deciding factor is not known. Whatever the case, it seems clear that a DTP might serve as tool for helping principals and human resource personnel choose candidates for positions, particularly when it comes down to selecting the appropriate candidate for a position. In some areas, the competition for certain positions is so high that having a DTP might help tip a decision in a teacher candidate's favor. However, simply having a DTP may not be the deciding factor in landing a job.

Teachers applied most of the technology skills learned while developing their DTP with the exception of web site design skills. Although this study supports previous research that demonstrates teacher candidates learn technology skills (see Barrett, 1999, 2000; Kilbane & Milman, 2003; McKinney, 1998; Milman, 1999, 2000), it raises questions about the extent to which these skills are learned and might be applied later on as teachers take on the full responsibility of teaching.

In general, teachers' beliefs about DTPs were quite positive. Teachers reported that creating DTPs was very beneficial to them and also potentially for preservice and inservice teachers—beliefs that carried through even years after creating DTPs as preservice teachers. It seems that school districts have the potential for tapping into these positive beliefs and using DTPs as tools for professional development.

The systemic obstacles that impeded updating and maintaining DTPs are difficult to tackle. These are many of the same barriers that teachers have generally and historically encountered for incorporating technology in their classrooms (Hadley & Sheingold, 1993; Marcinkiewicz, 1994; U.S. Congress Office of Technology and Assessment, 1995; Willis, 1993). Until these barriers are overcome, implementations of DTPs by practicing, inservice teachers will likely remain minimal.

SUMMARY

So, what happens after preservice teacher education students graduate with regards to the DTPs they had created as preservice teachers? It is evident that the participants in this study continued to value their experiences of creating DTPs even as they moved into teaching or other positions. However, out of the 20 participants in this study, only one was actively working on updating her DTP, albeit on disk. Two others were required to maintain print-based portfolios by their states for licensure purposes, but it was unclear whether DTPs would be accepted over traditional, print-based ones.

Participants described a number of systemic conditions that acted as barriers to updating and maintaining their DTPs: lack of time, support, resources, incentives, knowledge, and curricular demands to address state standards. And, all of the participants—except for one—indicated that they would like to update their DTP if they had the time. Several also indicated that they lacked knowledge about how to update their DTPs even though this was a topic discussed during one of the class sessions. No matter how much experience a teacher has, finding the time and resources for any type of professional development is a challenge. Yet, it is also important to comprehend how these barriers seem magnified, particularly during the first few years of teaching.

IMPLICATIONS

Whether teacher educators recognize it or not, they are planting the seeds for using DTPs as professional development tools. Thus, teacher educators are obligated to find ways to build bridges between SCDEs and school districts to help teachers continue revising and updating their DTPs—even after they graduate—so they may continue reflecting on their practice in meaningful, purposeful ways. Why plant the seeds without providing the needed nourishment to grow? The question remains as to how to build opportunities for teachers to keep using DTPs as continuous professional development tools, even after they complete programs in SCDEs. The use of "turnkey" solutions (Kilbane & Milman, 2005) such as Chalk and Wire's ePortfolio (see http://www.chalkandwire.com/eportfolio/) or Taskstream's Web Folio (see http://www.taskstream.com/), among the many options available, may address the need to update a DTP considering these products allow teachers to create DTPs easily and quickly, but the question still remains how teachers will find the time, incentives, and resources to maintain and update their DTPs using such systems in light of the demands to address state standards and day-to-day demands.

RECOMMENDATIONS FOR FUTURE RESEARCH AND PRACTICE

Based on the findings of this study and research design, there are several recommendations for future research and practice:

1. Conduct longitudinal studies using multiple and mixed methods that provide large-scale, rich descriptions of the application, implementation, and impact of DTPs through the years—it seems that performing single method (e.g., only quantitative or only qualitative studies) does not provide researchers with the opportunity to understand the larger context in which teachers teach and also gather data from such a dispersed, diverse population in an efficient, concise way
2. Provide a support system (e.g., incentives and "just in time" training about how to update a DTP), particularly during the induction period for teachers to continue developing, revising, and adding to their DTPs
3. Provide easy, free, and/or inexpensive ways to house DTPs in the long term
4. Build bridges between SCDEs and school districts for educating one another about the benefits and challenges of DTPs

5. Document and disseminate research findings so that others may build on this growing field that is still in its infancy.

REFERENCES

American Council on Education. (1999). *To touch the future: Transforming the way teachers are taught.* Washington, D.C.: Author.

Barrett, H. (1999). *Using Technology to Support Alternative Assessment and Electronic Portfolios.* Retrieved February 22, 2002, from http://transition.alaska.edu/www/portfolios.html.

Barrett, H. (2000, April). Create your own electronic portfolio. *Learning & Leading with Technology, 27*(7), 14–21.

Borko, H., Michalec, P., Timmons, M., & Siddle, J. (1997, November-December). Student teaching portfolios: A tool for promoting reflective practice. *Journal of Teacher Education, 48*(5), 345–357.

CEO Forum of Educational Technology. (1999, February). *Professional development: A link to better learning.* Retrieved February 22, 2002, from http://www.ceoforum.org/reports.cfm?RID=2.

Cresswell, J. W., Plano Clark, V. L., Gutmann, M. L., & Hanson, W. E. (2003). Advanced mixed methods research designs. In A. Tashakkori, & C. Teddlie (Eds.), *Handbook of mixed methods in social & behavioral research,* (pp. 209–240). Thousand Oaks, CA: Sage Publications.

Darling-Hammond, L. (Ed.). (1992, September). *Model standards for beginning teaching licensing and development: A resource for state dialogue.* Interstate New Teacher Assessment and Support Consortium, Council of Chief State School Officers, Washington, DC.

Dietz, M. (1995). Using portfolios as a framework for professional development. *Journal of Staff Development, 16,* 40–43.

Erickson, F. (1986). Qualitative methods in research on teaching. In M. C. Wittrock (Ed.), *Handbook of research on teaching,* (3rd ed., pp. 119–161).

Green, J., & Smyser, S. (1996). *The teacher portfolio: A strategy for professional development and evaluation.* Lancaster, PA: Technomic.

Hadley, M., & Sheingold, K. (1993, May). Commonalties and distinctive patterns in teachers' integration of computers. *American Journal of Education, 101,* 261–315.

International Society for Technology in Education. (1999). *Will new teachers be prepared to teach in a Digital Age? A national survey on information technology in teacher education.* Santa Monica, CA: Milken Exchange on Education Technology. Retrieved February 22, 2002, from http://www.milkenexchange.org/research/iste_results.html.

Jackson, D. (1998). *Developing student generated computer portfolios.* Paper presented at the ninth annual conference of the Society for Information Technology and Teacher Education, Washington, D.C.

Kemper, E. A., Stringfield, S., & Teddlie, C. (2003). Mixed methods sampling strategies in social sciences research. In A. Tashakkori, & C. Teddlie (Eds.), *Hand-*

book of mixed methods in social & behavioral research (pp. 273–296). Thousand Oaks, CA: Sage.

Kilbane, C. R., & Milman, N. B. (2003). *The digital teaching portfolio handbook: a how-to guide for educators.* Boston: Allyn & Bacon.

Kilbane, C. R., & Milman, N. B. (2005). *Understanding the digital teaching portfolio process: A workbook for teachers.* Boston: Allyn & Bacon.

Loughran, J., & Corrigan, D. (1995). Teaching portfolios: A strategy for developing learning and teaching in preservice teacher education. *Teaching and Teacher Education, 11,* 565–577.

Lyons, N. (1998a). Portfolios and their consequences: Developing as a reflective practitioner. In Lyons, N. (Ed.), *With portfolio in hand: Validating the new teacher professionalism* (pp. 23–37). New York: Teachers College Press.

Lyons, N. (1998b, Winter). Reflection in teaching: Can it be developmental? A portfolio perspective. *Teacher Education Quarterly, 25*(1), 115–127.

Marcinkiewicz, H. R. (1994, Winter). Computers and teachers: Factors influencing computer use in the classroom. *Journal of Research on Computing in Education 26,*(2), 220–236.

McKinney, M. (1998, Winter). Preservice teachers' electronic portfolios: Integrating technology, self-assessment, and reflection. *Teacher Education Quarterly, 25*(1), 85–103.

Milman, N. B. (1999). *Web-based electronic teaching portfolios for preservice teachers.* Proceedings of the Society for Information Technology and Teacher Education. San Antonio, TX: Association for the Advancement of Computing in Education.

Milman, N. B. (2000, April). *Electronic teaching portfolios and the development of reflection and technology competence in preservice teacher education students.* Invited Panel Presentation presented at the American Educational Research Association Annual Meeting, New Orleans, LA.

Mokhtari, K., Yellin, D., Bull, K., & Montgomery, D. (1996, September-October). Portfolio assessment in teacher education: Impact on preservice teachers' knowledge and attitudes. *Journal of Teacher Education, 47*(4), 245–262.

Morse, J. M. (2003). Principles of mixed methods and multimethod research design. In A. Tashakkori, & C. Teddlie (Eds.), *Handbook of mixed methods in social & behavioral research,* (pp. 189–208). Thousand Oaks, CA: Sage Publications.

National Commission on Teaching & America's Future. (1996). *What matters most: Teaching for America's future.* New York: Author.

National Council for Accreditation of Teacher Education. (1997). *Technology and the new professional teacher: Preparing for the 21st century classroom.* Washington, DC: Author.

Newman, I., Ridenour, C. S., Newman, C., & DeMarco, G. M. P. (2003). A typology of research purposes and its relationship to mixed methods. In A. Tashakkori, & C. Teddlie (Eds.), *Handbook of mixed methods in social & behavioral research* (pp. 167–188). Thousand Oaks, CA: Sage.

Persichitte, K. A., Tharp, D. D., & Caffarella, E. P. (1996). *The use of technology by schools, colleges, and departments of education 1996.* Washington, D.C.: American Association of Colleges for Teacher Education.

Shulman, L. (1998). Teacher portfolios: A theoretical activity. In N. Lyons (Ed.), *With portfolio in hand: Validating the new teacher professionalism* (pp. 23–37). New York: Teachers College Press.

Stroble, E. (1995). Portfolio pedagogy: Assembled evidence and unintended consequences. *Teacher Education, 7*(2), 97–102.

Strudler, N., & Wetzel, K. (2005). The diffusion of electronic portfolios in teacher education: Issues of initiation and implementation. *Journal of Research on Technology in Education, 37*(4), 411–433.

Tashakkori, A., & Teddlie, C. (1998). *Mixed methodology: Combining qualitative and quantitative approaches.* Thousand Oaks, CA: Sage.

Teddlie, C., & Tashakkori, A. (2003). Major issues and controversies in the use of mixed methods in the social and behavioral sciences. In A. Tashakkori, & C. Teddlie (Eds.), *Handbook of mixed methods in social & behavioral research* (pp. 3–50). Thousand Oaks, CA: Sage Publications.

U.S. Congress, Office of Technology Assessment. (1995). *Teachers and technology: Making the connection.* Washington, DC: U.S. Government Printing Office.

Wade, R., & Yarbrough, D. (1996). Portfolios: A tool for reflective thinking in teacher education? *Teaching and Teacher Education, 12,* 63–79.

Willis, J. (1993). What conditions encourage technology use? It depends on the context. *Computers in the Schools, 9*(4) 13–32.

Willis, J. W., & Mehlinger, H. D. (1996). Information technology and teacher education. In J. Sikula (Ed.), *Handbook of research on teacher education* (pp. 978–1029). New York: Macmillan Library Reference.

Wray, S. (2001). *The impact of using teaching portfolios on student teachers' professional development.* Paper presented at the American Educational Research Association Annual Meeting, Seattle, WA.

Zidon, M. (1996, Spring). Portfolios in preservice teacher education: What the students say. *Action in Teacher Education, 18*(1) 59–70.

CHAPTER 6

FOCUSING ON CHANGE IN INDIVIDUAL TEACHERS' PRACTICES OVER TIME

An Evaluation Model for Electronic Portfolios in Teacher Education

Pete Adamy
University of Rhode Island

Natalie Milman
George Washington University

The authors in this volume make either the argument or the assumption that the use of electronic portfolios as a performance-based assessment tool for teacher education is a value-added practice. This value consists of their functionality as a means for increasing reflective practice by pre-service teachers; as a method for collecting, organizing, and analyzing the outcomes based data produced in the course of a student teacher's experi-

Evaluating Electronic Portfolios in Teacher Education, pages 111–117
Copyright © 2009 by Information Age Publishing
111

ence; and, when implemented appropriately, as an aid for data collection and analysis in the accreditation process.

The use of portfolios for outcomes-based assessment in teacher education is a practice with a history of effective use (Darling-Hammond, 2006; Darling-Hammond, Hammerness, Grossman, Rust, & Shulman, 2005; Shulman, 1998). However, when looking at electronic portfolios as a common assessment tool in teacher education, it is important to temper assumptions with an appropriate level of skepticism. There are findings in the research literature indicating that technology, used appropriately, can enrich and expand learning and instruction by strengthening basic skills, motivating students, connecting learning to real-world activities (Lemke & Coughlin, 1998), raising test scores, making the learning process more efficient, and improving attitudes towards learning and self-concept (Schacter, 1999). However, in the current climate of increased accountability for teachers, electronic portfolios present schools, colleges, and departments of education (SCDE's) and researchers with the challenge of establishing validity to a convincing degree (Adamy, 2004). Wilkerson and Lang (2003) have suggested that the use of portfolios in teacher education is problematic. Given the high stakes nature of many contemporary standards-based outcomes assessments, in which a student's eligibility for professional licensure may be confirmed or denied, it is vital for SCDE's to ensure that such assessments have established, demonstrable levels of validity and reliability that are sufficient to justify such decisions.

Evaluators are typically charged with considering validity at internal and external levels (Campbell & Stanley, 1966). External validity focuses on variables of generalizability. Since portfolios are typically defined as tools for individual, formative assessments, the ability to generalize beyond the individual portfolio user, and thus the importance of external validity, is minimized. This leaves the evaluator to focus on internal validity. The real challenge is to determine the extent to which portfolios enable instructors to make accurate conclusions about what students have learned and can do.

Reliability is not an appropriate concern for electronic portfolios, because narrowing the scope sufficiently to increase consistency takes the focus away from the portfolio process to a more narrowly defined product. Portfolios are more appropriate for measuring individual growth than program effectiveness (Reynolds, 2000; Reis & Kidd Villaume, 2002).

The term portfolio, whether for teaching, learning, and/or assessment, will have different meanings and purposes for different people. For results of any study to be useful, it is therefore vital for practitioners and researchers to define specifically what the term means to them (Adamy, 2004; Barrett, 2005). As demonstrated by the authors in this volume, the concept of a portfolio for learning and assessment can have multiple meanings and implementations, and all of the authors spend time elaborating what the electronic portfolio tool means in their particular contexts. From an evaluation perspective, this act of definition is crucial for any teacher education program going through the process of adopting an electronic portfolio system.

A THEORETICAL FOCUS

Shulman (1998) has referred to the creation of portfolios as a theoretical act, meaning that "what is declared worth documenting, worth reflecting on, what is deemed to be portfolio-worthy" is a reflection of one's assessment philosophy (p. 24). Several of the authors in this volume highlight the notion that the process of implementing, assessing, and evaluating electronic portfolios is also, necessarily, a theoretical act. As such, it makes sense to approach electronic portfolio assessment with a clear understanding of the theoretical basis that underlies the decision to use electronic portfolios as an assessment tool. Any attempt to do so without such an understanding, runs the risk of becoming a process devoid of meaning, particularly in relation to the reasons for engaging in outcomes based assessment in the first place (Wetzel & Strudler, 2005). In the more specific terms of validity, theoretical consistency among stakeholders can help to maximize the validity of assessments by providing a coherent and consistent structure with which tasks and assessments can be aligned.

Several of the authors in this volume present models of electronic portfolio systems and their use that are structured according to a theoretical framework that provides a clear focus for users at all levels. Ultimately, however, the focus of each model is on the individual and his or her development in the teaching environment. Consistent with a focus on internal validity, these evaluation models focus on learning and development at the individual level, combining this individuality with theoretical coherence to enhance the rigor and consistency with which such systems can be evaluated.

In chapter two, Recesso, Hannafin, Wang, Deaton, Rich, and Shepherd present the Evidential Reasoning & Decision Making (ERDM) method for portfolio assessment for teacher education, which enables a direct link between teaching practices and related goals and objectives. This method allows teachers to examine complex events and interactions to identify causes and effects in their practice. From a theoretical perspective, ERDM is developmental and formative in nature, facilitating examination at pre-service, induction, and professional levels. Portfolio-based ERDM enables teachers at all three levels to evaluate their performance against standards and competencies. The authors outline a four-stage ERDM process that provides structure for the teachers. The theoretical framework inherent in this four-stage process provides structure for conducting ERDM in complex environments.

Bartlett proposes a five-step evaluation approach. In this model, the evaluator begins with an assessment of the candidates' work, and then moves beyond to evaluate their perceptions of the task, perceptions of the advantages and disadvantages of electronic portfolios, changes in candidates' technology knowledge and attitudes, and their use of technology as beginning teachers. This approach helps ensure consistency among evaluators, and uses data from the electronic portfolio users to help increase the validity of evaluation results through triangulation and member-checking.

Beck and Bear focus on reflection as the central activity of the e-folio user, and analysis of reflection as a process in the teaching cycle of planning, instruction, and assessment. They view reflection as a cognitive tool that teachers can use to connect planning, instruction, and assessment in their daily practice. They propose a theoretical model of reflection with five dimensions:

1. General reflective skill
2. Assessment reflection
3. Reflections linking assessment and planning
4. Reflections on student work
5. Collaborative reflection

To build the soundness of the theoretical basis for using this type of assessment, the authors developed and implemented the Electronic Portfolio Assessment Scale (ePAS) to measure these five dimensions of reflection, and to make full use of empirical data and analysis. They then use their results to argue for the use of electronic portfolios as formative tools, focused specifically on improving professional practice and reflective skills, and against the effectiveness and validity of their use for summative assessment focused on program evaluation and improvement.

METHODOLOGICAL ISSUES

The remaining authors in this volume suggest techniques for the evaluation of portfolios for teacher educators. Havelock agrees with Wilkerson and Lang (2003) that the current climate in teacher education requires consistent and explicit linkage between electronic portfolio assessment outcomes and educational standards. In chapter four, he provides specific advice for an evaluator that begins with conversation that identifies: (a) the goals for the electronic portfolio, (b) the nature of evidence to be collected, (c) the procedure for collecting the evidence, (d) the nature of the finished product, and (e) the role of reflection in the electronic portfolio process. To maximize the potential for growth and development of prospective teachers, they suggest that electronic portfolio systems must be constructed to encourage and support meaningful reflection on practice. This is often in conflict with the use of electronic portfolios as accreditation tools. In addition, the author stresses flexibility in design, implementation, and refinement of the evaluation process; there must be adequate sampling and triangulation to avoid narrowness of focus, and an expanded timeline to allow the unfolding of the adoption process and for the evaluator to follow it.

From a methodological perspective, Havelock emphasizes the difficulty involved in using true experimental design for the evaluation of electronic portfolios, particularly in terms of the validity issues involved with selection of electronic portfolio tasks and products. He highlights full use of formative assessment results to inform adaptations in the electronic portfolio system, and the need for flexibility and a willingness to embrace emergent design as the most effective paradigm for electronic portfolio evaluation. This is stressed by Milman as well in chapter five, where a sequential mixed method (QUAN → QUAL) design is used in an electronic portfolio evaluation to emphasize that it is a "recursive, non-linear process". She suggests that such a mixed method approach is advantageous because it is sequential (in this study), which provides the opportunity to formulate additional questions that arise during the first quantitative phase of analysis, and ask these questions later in the qualitative phase, as well as enabling the evaluators to use triangulation in their analysis.

CONCLUSION

In addition to concordance with the literature on the importance of establishing high levels of validity in the evaluation of electronic portfolios, and the presentation of several variants of electronic portfolio systems in practice, the chapters in this volume, as a whole, present numerous strategies for effective evaluation:

- Be fully aware of the theoretical basis and objectives for the assessment system; why is this form of assessment being used in this context?
- Inform stakeholders of your evaluation methods. How will data be collected and analyzed? How will you report findings? Etc.
- Use theoretical frameworks to help structure your evaluation model, by aligning outcomes with research and/or standards based concepts, knowledge, and skills.

- Allow for emergent design and subsequent refinement of the evaluation model.
- Recognize the difficulties inherent in evaluating electronic portfolio systems at a programmatic level. Advise stakeholders that the nature of this form of assessment places internal validity at a higher level of importance than external validity or reliability.
- Because teaching occurs in a complex environment, use and evaluation of such an assessment system for teacher education should take place in an authentic and similarly complex context.
- Be fully aware of the population using the system. Make appropriate accommodations and/or modifications in the system and the evaluation model for learners with specific needs or disabilities.
- Use the evaluation as an opportunity for formative evaluation for students who are creating them. Several authors here argue that electronic portfolios are formative tools, and are less appropriate for the typical summative evaluation they are asked to perform.
- Involve the learners themselves in the evaluation through member-checking, to enhance internal validity and create the potential for triangulation.

In addition to these strategies for evaluation, the authors have asked questions regarding the ability of the electronic portfolio process to help teacher education students improve their technology skills and their ability to reflect on their practice, as well as the actual impact that such an assessment process has on their practice. Taking a broader perspective, we would ask one more question not considered here, but nevertheless important when examining the impact of electronic portfolios in teacher education: Does the use of this form of assessment and reflective activity lead beyond self-examination to changes in the teacher education students' planning, instruction, and assessment skills? This question will naturally lead to a more longitudinal evaluation model, in which it is reasonable to expect that follow-up data would be collected to determine the level at which these new teachers are using outcomes-based assessment, perhaps electronic portfolios, in their own classrooms.

REFERENCES

Adamy, P. (2004). Strategies for enhancing assessment with electronic portfolios. *Journal of Computing in Higher Education, 15*(2), 85–97.

Barrett, H. C. (2005). *Researching electronic portfolios and learner engagement.* Retrieved April, 2006, from http://www.electronicportfolios.com/reflect/whitepaper.pdf.

Campbell, D. T., & Stanley, J. C. (1966). *Experimental and quasi-experimental designs for research.* Chicago, IL: Rand McNally.

Darling-Hammond, L. (2006). *Powerful teacher education: Lessons from exemplary programs.* San Francisco: Jossey-Bass.

Darling-Hammond, L., Hammerness, K., Grossman, P., Rust, F., & Shulman, L. (2005). The design of teacher education programs. In L. Darling-Hammond & J. Bransford (Eds.), *Preparing teachers for a changing world: What teachers should learn and be able to do,* (pp. 390–441). San Francisco: Jossey-Bass.

Lemke, C., & Coughlin, E. C. (1998). *Technology in American schools: Seven dimensions for gauging progress.* Research study commissioned by the Milken Exchange on Education Technology. Santa Monica, CA.

Reis, N. K., & Kidd Villaume, S. (2002). The benefits, tensions, and visions of portfolios as a wide-scale assessment for teacher education. *Action in Teacher Education, 23*(4), 10–17.

Reynolds, N. (2000). *Portfolio teaching: A guide for instructors.* Boston, MA: Bedford/St. Martin's.

Schacter, J. (1999). *The impact of education technology on student achievement: What the most current research has to say.* Research study commissioned by the Milken Exchange on Education Technology, Santa Monica, CA.

Shulman, L. (1998). Teacher portfolios: A theoretical activity. In N. Lyons (Ed.). *With portfolio in hand: Validating the new teacher professionalism,* (pp. 23–37). New York: Teachers College Press.

Wetzel, K., & Strudler, N. (2005). The diffusion of electronic portfolios in teacher education: Next steps and recommendations from accomplished users. *Journal of Research on Technology in Education, 38*(2), 231–243.

Wilkerson, J. R., & Lang, W. S. (2003, December 3). Portfolios, the Pied Piper of teacher certification assessments: Legal and psychometric issues. *Education Policy Analysis Archives, 11*(45). Retrieved June, 2005 from http://epaa.asu.edu/epaa/v11n45/.

ABOUT THE CONTRIBUTORS

Pete Adamy is an Associate Professor of Education at the University of Rhode Island. His research and publications have been focused in the areas of improving teacher education through the integration of technology; the use of technology to enhance content area instruction and learning; and the use of technology in teaching and assessment, with a specific focus on teacher education.

Andrea Bartlett teaches undergraduate and graduate courses in literacy education in the Department of Curriculum Studies, University of Hawaii at Mānoa, Honolulu, HI. Her research focuses on maximizing technology in teacher education through electronic portfolios, effective use of laptops, and distance learning systems. Professor Bartlett would like to thank the Department of Educational Technology's LEI Aloha Preparing Tomorrow's Teachers to Use Technology (PT3) Grant staff for their assistance on this project.

Sharon L. Bear holds a Ph.D. in Education, with a specialty in Counseling Psychology, from the University of Southern California. As a Research Specialist in the Department of Education, University of California, Irvine, working under the "Preparing Tomorrow's Teachers to Use Technology" (PT3) grant, she specialized in the analysis of e-folios, with a focus on the self-reflection of preservice teachers.

Robert Beck is Visiting Professor of Education at Lawrence University and Professor Emeritus in the California Institute for Telecommunications and Information Technology at the University of California, Irvine. Beck has published a book, several book chapters and 30 articles in environmental and educational psychology. Recipient of two PT3 grants, he studied electronic

Evaluating Electronic Portfolios in Teacher Education, pages 119–120
Copyright © 2009 by Information Age Publishing
All rights of reproduction in any form reserved.

119

portfolios and computer supported collaborative learning in pre-service teachers. In experimental studies Beck and colleagues analyzed electronic discussions using social network analysis. Supported by the Spencer Foundation, he is currently researching the effects of diversity on electronic and face-to-face discussions.

Benjamin Deaton is a graduate research assistant at the University of Georgia.

Michael Hannafin is the Charles H. Wheatley-Georgia Research Alliance Eminent Scholar in Technology Enhanced Learning and Director of the Learning & Performance Support Laboratory at the University of Georgia. His research interest include psychological and pedagogical principles underlying student-centered learning, and the development of frameworks for designing and testing Open-Ended Learning Environments (OELEs) and Resource-Based Learning Environments (RBLEs).

Bruce Havelock has been conducting research and development in education technology in academic, public education, and business settings since 1995. This chapter emerged from his experience conducting program evaluation research for RMC Research Corporation in Denver, Colorado (www.rmcdenver.com) from 2002 to 2005. Bruce received his doctorate from the University of Washington just prior to joining RMC. He can be reached via havelock@post.harvard.edu.

Natalie B. Milman is an Assistant Professor of educational technology and curriculum and instruction with a joint appointment between the departments of Educational Leadership and Teacher Preparation and Special Education at George Washington University. Natalie's research interests include the study of digital portfolios, student engagement and learning through distance education, strategies for the integration of technology into the curriculum, and models for effective technology education and assessment at all academic levels. She has co-authored two books about digital portfolios.

Arthur Recesso is an Associate Research Scientist in the Learning & Performance Support Laboratory at the University of Georgia. His research interests include evidence interpretation for performance assessment, educational policy, and educational leadership.

Peter Rich is a graduate research assistant at the University of Georgia.

Craig Shepherd is a graduate research assistant at the University of Georgia.

Feng Wang is a graduate research assistant at the University of Georgia.

**SCHOOL OF EDUCATION
CURRICULUM LABORATORY
UM-DEARBORN**

Printed in the United States
138713LV00002B/1/P